BOYS in POVERTY

A Framework for Understanding Dropout

Ruby K. PAYNE / Paul D. SLOCUMB

Solution Tree | Press

a division of
Solution Tree

555 North Morton Street
Bloomington, IN 47404

800.733.6786 (toll free) / 812.336.7700
FAX: 812.336.7790

email: info@solution-tree.com
solution-tree.com

Printed in the United States of America

14 13 12 11   2 3 4 5

FSC
Mixed Sources
Product group from well-managed
forests and other controlled sources

Cert no. SW-COC-002283
www.fsc.org
© 1996 Forest Stewardship Council

Library of Congress Cataloging-in-Publication Data

Payne, Ruby K.
   Boys in poverty : a framework for understanding dropout / Ruby K. Payne, Paul D. Slocumb.
       p. cm.
   Includes bibliographical references and index.
   ISBN 978-1-935542-22-3 (perfect bound) -- ISBN 978-1-935249-86-3 (library edition) 1. High school dropouts--United States--Statistics--Methodology. 2. Poor children--Services for--United States--Evaluation. 3. Dropout behavior, Prediction of. I. Slocumb, Paul D. II. Title.
   LC146.6.P39 2011
   371.2'91308624--dc22
                                    2010021611

Solution Tree
Jeffrey C. Jones, CEO & President

Solution Tree Press
President: Douglas M. Rife
Publisher: Robert D. Clouse
Vice President of Production: Gretchen Knapp
Managing Production Editor: Caroline Wise
Senior Production Editor: Edward Levy
Proofreader: Rachel Rosolina
Cover and Text Designer: Orlando Angel

Acknowledgments

We would like to thank the many, many teachers throughout the United States who have shared their experiences with us. We learn from them every day.

We also would like to thank: Rúben Pérez, who added real-world richness to this book with his firsthand stories of at-risk boys; Cheryl Sattler, a tireless and gifted researcher, who assisted us in the sourcing and citation work; Dan Shenk, our faithful editor, whose expertise and experience have helped us once again complete a challenging project; Peg Conrad, who worked to coordinate multiple individuals through countless revisions and changes; Jesse Conrad, who checked and rechecked the references; and our friends at Solution Tree, who went out on a limb in their belief that we have something to say that will help boys from poverty have better lives.

Solution Tree Press would like to thank the following reviewers:

Marc Barlow
Title I Coordinator
Monte Vista High School
Spring Valley, California

Elizabeth R. Cocina
Dean of Students
McReynolds Middle School
Houston, Texas

Stacie Cook Emert
Principal
Wheeler Elementary School
Tucson, Arizona

Elaine Fahrner
Principal
The Academy at Old Cockrill
Nashville, Tennessee

Gayle C. Manchin
First Lady of West Virginia
Charleston, West Virginia

Paul V. Mitchell
Principal
Colonial High School
Orlando, Florida

Michael G. Nygaard
Assistant Principal
Fargo South High School
Fargo, North Dakota

Jacqueline M. Wyant
Assistant Principal
West High School
Sioux City, Iowa

Wendell Waukau
Superintendent
Menominee Indian School District
Keshena, Wisconsin

Elizabeth Zilkowski
Ninth-Grade Academy Leader
Manual High School
Peoria, Illinois

Christina Wilkes
Eighth-Grade Science Teacher
Adams Middle School
Tampa, Florida

Table of Contents

About the Authors

Ruby K. Payne is an author, speaker, publisher, business owner, and career educator. She is an expert on the mindsets of economic classes and on crossing socioeconomic lines in education and work.

Ruby's work stems from more than thirty years of firsthand experience in the public schools as a high school department head, principal, and central-office administrator of staff development. She became known for helping students from all economic backgrounds achieve academic success.

Ruby received her BA from Goshen College in Indiana, earned a master's degree in English literature from Western Michigan University in Kalamazoo, and obtained her doctorate in educational leadership and policy from Loyola University in Chicago, Illinois.

She has written or coauthored more than a dozen books. Her foundational work, *A Framework for Understanding Poverty* (1996), has sold more than a million copies. As founder and president of aha! Process, Inc., she has created more than a hundred publications in all media. Ruby travels extensively and has presented her work throughout North America, and in Europe, Australia, China, and India. She presents a variety of workshops that include strategies for successfully raising student achievement and overcoming economic class barriers. She has a grown son, Tom.

Paul D. Slocumb has been a professional educator since 1966, serving as a secondary-school teacher, adjunct teacher at the university level, instructional supervisor, director of curriculum, campus administrator, and deputy superintendent for curriculum and instruction. Throughout his career, Paul has had the opportunity to work with students and families from a wide variety of backgrounds. These experiences came together in *Hear*

Our Cry: Boys in Crisis (2004), which discusses the emotional abyss faced by many boys, and how to address it.

After addressing curricular and instructional issues professionally for more than thirty years, Paul began observing and working directly with the academic, social, and emotional issues of boys. Since 1997, he has been writing and consulting on the needs of students from poverty for aha! Process, Inc. He coauthored *Removing the Mask: Giftedness in Poverty* (2000) with Ruby Payne and is a past president of the Texas Association for the Gifted and Talented.

Paul received his BA from the University of Houston and earned a master's degree from Sam Houston University and a doctorate from the University of Houston. Residing in the Houston area, he has two grown children, Eric and Schelli.

Foreword

by Michael Gurian

Nearly every issue our society faces today intersects with the demographic group referred to as "boys in poverty." Advocates of legislative action on healthcare, military, prison, and school reform; on family development; on media practices; and on safety in society can powerfully assess future success by asking, "How will this legislation affect the healthy development of boys in poverty?" Because this demographic exists in urban and rural areas and everywhere in between, and because of the significant stress these boys are under, boys in poverty account for the majority of our violent crime, drug trade, and juvenile incarceration rates. Many of these boys are homeless, have no access to healthcare, are victims of violence on our streets and in our schools, and end up in prison. They try to survive to adulthood without crucial familial attachments and often derive their role models from media imagery—which is itself a problematic survival technique.

At the same time, anyone who has worked with these boys sees in them, especially when they first enter school, an inward pull to discover aspects of self—such as identity, purpose, and motivation—that could contribute to their success, along with a pull toward education. All of us see a light in their eyes from early on, but we see that light grow dimmer in the next few years. Although we know that school can be a haven for these boys, many of them decide it is not a place in which they can learn survival skills or thrive, for those are their highest priorities. These are the boys who drop out by the time they reach middle or high school, creating a crisis of male dropouts that costs our society tens of billions of dollars.

If these are some of the sad complaints we all share regarding the state of boys in poverty, what are the solutions? You will find many powerful answers in the wisdom, experience, and pedagogical work of Ruby Payne and Paul Slocumb. After reading the first half of *Boys in Poverty,* I made this note in a margin: "They [the authors] show us that our collective educational and social instinct is true: if we can educate boys raised in poverty to become successful men, we will do something not only educationally mandated, but also socially and personally heroic." Since this is not the kind of note that generally makes the final cut into a foreword or academic article (it can seem overblown), I crossed it out and kept reading, noting the book's specific ideas and practical strategies.

Over and over again, however, I found myself returning to that sentence. Having now finished reading the text, I am writing it into this foreword. *Boys in Poverty* is a crucial book for educators and for our ongoing social debates. The authors prove that dealing with the educational needs of boys in poverty is a heroic task, one for which there are now turnaround strategies and practical tools that can seriously shape our work as teachers. Thankfully, the strategies and tools provided in this book gain their credentials not only from being utilized and evaluated in schools, but also from the personal experiences of Payne and Slocumb, who come at their topic with decades of professional experience, as well as their own childhood stories of poverty.

Both survived significant poverty—a poverty each of them also saw in the eyes of their fathers. Both grew up seeing that boys, young men, and grown men are affected by poverty in gender-specific ways. This realization led the authors to look carefully at the academic, scientific, and wisdom-of-practice research available on boys in schools. In the process, they discovered that:

- Boys and girls learn differently, in a number of important ways.

- Our teachers are often unaware of the effects of these differences on teaching and learning across the curriculum.

- Our educational systems are often mismatched with the way boys learn, unconsciously assuming boys will or should learn well in whatever verbal and cognitive model they're taught.

- Lack of awareness and systemic mismatches like these often significantly impede boys' success as a group and as individuals, increasing dropout rates.

- These factors are exacerbated when poverty is included in the research.

In making their discoveries, Payne and Slocumb checked and rechecked their research. *Boys in Poverty* also includes an important literature review on a diversity of relevant topics, such as the sciences of nature and nurture, international research on boys and schools, the financial effects of dropout rates, the effects of bad nutrition on boys' learning abilities, and many others. In each case, Payne and Slocumb hone research findings to the specific demographic of boys in poverty.

The authors then move to practical interventions every teacher and school can utilize. In their collective seventy years of professional experience in schools, Payne and Slocumb have developed leading-edge, practical strategies for increasing teacher effectiveness with children raised in poverty. Both authors have noted how important teachers were in their own journeys through poverty, and both have worked for decades to help teachers become decisively important in the lives of impoverished boys and girls.

The authors' emphasis on practicalities is one of the finest features of this book. The strategies and interventions presented directly target the goals of increasing teacher effectiveness and helping keep impoverished boys in school. While providing wisdom on many educational practices that can help all children—boys and girls, gifted and nongifted learners, from all socioeconomic groups—Payne and Slocumb always make sure to link their practical strategies to the goal of lowering dropout rates for boys in poverty. This targeted approach leads to credible, practical outcomes. By staying on task, the authors provide specific interventions and tools for improving four key areas of a boy's development: physical, emotional, cognitive, and social. Specifically, Payne and Slocumb show educators practical ways to bond with boys raised in poverty, alter classrooms to fit boys' learning styles, become sensitive to their hidden signals, alter discipline systems to best nurture these boys' spirits, and help school districts systemically change teacher training toward knowledge of boy-specific success strategies.

In deciding to write this book, Payne and Slocumb set a heroic task for themselves. They knew what every other professional knows: schools can't do all that is needed to solve issues of boys raised in poverty. Teachers can't raise boys—that is still the job of parents and extended family members. But Payne and Slocumb also know that schools that succeed are those that become like an extended family to the boy. If we adjust our schools and classrooms toward best practices in educating boys in poverty, we can create a place where these boys can survive and thrive—where they can develop a great deal of their healthy identity, discover in themselves a work ethic of the highest quality, and become motivated toward the success goals every human being in a democratic society deserves to pursue and attain.

As you turn the pages of this book, I hope you will feel yourself taken into the crucial story it tells. Payne and Slocumb are wise guides on this journey, and I am personally and professionally thankful to them for letting me walk with them down this difficult and ultimately hopeful road.

Michael Gurian is cofounder of the Gurian Institute (www.gurianinstitute .com) and author of *The Minds of Boys*, *The Wonder of Boys*, and *Boys and Girls Learn Differently!*

Preface

Why, you are probably asking, would a white, middle-class woman care about boys in poverty and whether they drop out or not—especially since she grew up in a very closed, conservative religious group with a gender bias against women in leadership roles? Why isn't she talking about girls dropping out and working on behalf of girls? What experiences and thinking brought her to this book?

My father was the third generation of a German immigrant family and grew up in poverty in a farming community in Iowa. His father died when he was a year old. My father was also a minister, dairy and grain farmer, and seventh- and eighth-grade teacher. My mother grew up middle class in Colorado and had two years of college when she married my father. Because they had no assets when they started out, they began farming.

From an early age, I learned to work. I took care of the younger children while my mother helped farm. I learned to drive a tractor at nine years old. I cooked breakfast on school days for my siblings so that my mother could help milk the cows. When I was eleven years old, my parents bought an old farm house that was in the way of the developing Interstate 71. From that lumber, we built a 1600-square-foot house. We all pounded nails, mixed mortar, helped with the drywall, painted. We also had a garden. At the time, I thought it was a curse because of all the work, but I now understand that it gave us access to healthy, good food.

And we went to church, and we went to church, and we went to church.

I *loved* school, and I always knew I was going to be a teacher. In fact, a couple of times the first-grade teacher had to have a "come to Jesus" meeting with me, because I thought *I* was the teacher. I never played with dolls. Instead, I sat them in a row and taught them, and as I got older, I taught my siblings. They were, of course, the worst class a teacher could have. They fought with each other, talked back to the teacher, criticized the lesson, and complained to the authorities (my parents). They absolutely refused discipline in any form, so the only way to teach them was to keep them interested. I learned early on that teaching was, to a great extent, about keeping the students interested and entertained.

One of my brothers had an absolutely terrible time in school, and that was my first experience with how very painful school can be for some people—and how much one teacher can ruin a life. My father, because he had been a teacher himself, had a rule that you could not complain about or confront a teacher. (At that time, the Mennonite religion was fairly clear that the woman was to obey the man, so this rule was not questioned.) This teacher, Mr. Bach, had my brother for two years in a row—fourth and fifth grades. He would taunt my brother with "Go stand in the corner. Let the class see how stupid you are," and "Let's all talk about how many you missed on this test." It was an absolutely horrendous experience—so much so that his classmates would go home from school crying and tell their parents what happened. At night, he and my mother also cried, and this went on for two years. To this day, my brother has no confidence in his abilities, in spite of all the effort to mitigate the damage.

For all of that, my family was very stable, my mother was an excellent disciplinarian, and my father had a great sense of humor, loved people, and was an excellent storyteller. My parents worked hard and instilled in their children the concepts of work, diligence, integrity, and religion.

I was always a curious child. (Once, my mother, in a fit of frustration, said to me, "Well, if you don't know, it's certainly not your fault!") I graduated salutatorian of my class and went on to Goshen College, a Mennonite school that required students to live in a third-world country for a trimester to study poverty and perform service. For three and a half months, I lived in Haiti, where only about 30 percent of the people have any education at all. It was my first exposure to extreme poverty. From that experience, I became committed to public education. Without education, I saw, a person is often condemned to a world of violence, superstition, rumors, misunderstandings, manipulation, and threats. In Haiti I also learned that when the man's world is unstable, so is the woman's, so is the child's, and so is the community.

During my junior year of college, I met my former husband, Frank. He was a mix of Caucasian and Cherokee and grew up in extreme poverty, living in a mostly white neighborhood next to the railroad tracks. He was a day student at Goshen College while working at night in a factory. Frank's dad had died when he was six, and his mother had five children. I met him through his brother, who was also working at the Holiday Inn, where I worked three days a week as a waitress. That is when I encountered giftedness and poverty.

Frank had three siblings with IQs over 150. One has a photographic memory. I had never met a family that had read so much or had such sophisticated vocabulary. I also learned how devastating the school experience can be to students in poverty and, even when they are very bright, how alienated and isolated from school they feel because of the social isolation and the very different daily experience that comes with poverty. To hide the silence and humiliation, there is often a very aggressive and disgusted approach to middle-class institutions.

Generational poverty always has as one of its roots either no work or unstable work. In lots of research, male identity is often tied to work and the ability to provide. Observing Frank's neighborhood was the second time in my life I had seen what happened when men did not have stable work. (The first was Haiti.) Work provides stability, meaning, structure, social interaction, and learning (sometimes). To have stable work in America now, you have to be educated.

Three times in my marriage, Frank was out of work, even though he had four years of college and was nine hours from a degree in biology. I saw what unemployment did to identity, stability, and personal worth. I also knew that had there been better support, more understanding of the hidden rules, and an understanding of the paper world of college, Frank would have had a degree. Yet he turned down offers for promotion because he did "not want to be a company man"—one of the hidden rules of poverty.

From the outset of my career as an educator, I met many superintendents, principals, and teachers, and they all told stories—particularly if they thought you could keep your mouth shut. A superintendent in a small rural Texas town once told me of a sixth-grade boy from a very poor family who quit coming to school. This boy had built a gasoline engine from aluminum Coke cans, and the engine worked. The superintendent had tears in his eyes as he talked about the incredible loss of talent and his inability to get this student to return to school. His story clarified for me what I had seen so often in Frank's family and neighborhood—the unbelievable loss of talent and the incredible difficulty.

In a postmodern society, in order to have stable work and be a provider—whether you are male or female—you have to be educated. However, we are not educating our boys very well at all, and they are dropping out. When you are not educated, how do you have work? You don't—or you have intermittent work and never get to develop your full potential.

Then how do you make a living? Often illegally. And where do you end up? Sometimes in prison. Who pays—emotionally, economically, sociologically—for that underdeveloped talent? Everyone does, in every way.

It is, quite simply, enough. There is no need for it to be this way. That is the purpose of this book.

—Ruby Payne

Young children have to deal with the cards that their parents and life have dealt them. I grew up in a family of eight in rural poverty. Both my parents were products of generational poverty. My mom was one of five, and all the girls dropped out of school in the eighth grade and went to work. My father was the only one of his siblings to graduate from high school. He didn't graduate until he was twenty-one, and he would never have finished at all had it not been for sports. The coaches were happy to have a twenty-year-old football player competing against sixteen-year-olds.

My parents had six children, of whom I was the second, in an eight-year span. Trying to make a living doing construction in a small, rural Illinois town was difficult, and my father passed his frustration on to us. He was physically abusive to the three boys in the family, especially to my older brother and me, and verbally abusive to my mother. I can remember going to middle school and not wanting to take my shirt off in physical education class so no one would see the stripes on my back from the belt my dad had used on me the night before. My mother was more psychologically than physically abusive.

I was also the victim of sexual abuse and sexual exploitation by people brought into the home, another source of great shame as a child. There were secrets—and no one to talk to about them. School was the one place where I could go and feel safe. I was never late, and from first through twelfth grade I missed only three days of school, when I got the flu. School was safe—a haven, actually—and I saw teachers I wanted to be like.

I also grew up in a fundamentalist Christian environment. I went to church with my family every Sunday morning and evening, as well as Wednesday and Friday evenings. Not going was not an option. It was a highly emotional environment, filled with hellfire and brimstone. Most of the members of this small church were people with little education, but one was an elementary school teacher who told me about her students and her job. Once she told me she was working on her master's thesis (whatever that was), and showed me the trunk of her car filled with books she was using for her research.

I can recall as a small child hearing my mother praying late at night to provide for her children. With tears running down her cheeks, she would ask God to provide food and clothing for her children. Consequently, I learned very early not to ask for anything. If I wanted it, I knew I would have to get it myself. This sensitive child didn't want to be part of the problem. That paid off later on—it created independence, determination, and a work ethic that would drive me for a lifetime.

When I was sixteen, I took a part-time job a block from the high school, sweeping floors and stocking shelves at a men's clothing store. On Saturday, I got to sell the merchandise. I bought my first sport coat so I could wear it on Saturday. My employer allowed me to pay $5 a week out of my $14.05-a-week paycheck on my $25 purchase.

Just as I was graduating, a new community college opened next to the store, and for fifty dollars a semester, I began college. My higher-education journey had begun. After my second year, the University of Houston became a state-supported university, so I enrolled and paid my tuition (again just fifty dollars per semester). I had decided to become a teacher.

Looking back on that journey amazes me to this day. The proximity of the schools for this young, poor boy was crucial. Had the community college not started that year, had the university not received state funding, my college education would have either been delayed or I wouldn't have finished college. I always felt there was a grand plan for me. Ruby Payne, my colleague in the writing of this book, talks about having a sense of destiny being an important personal resource. Well, I had a sense of destiny. I knew education was the way out, and I was fortunate to have teachers who saw potential in me when I did not always see that potential in myself.

My second year as a teacher, the district closed its all-black school, and those students came to our school. Times were tense all across the country in the mid-1960s. That spring, in the commons area, students threw Coke bottles, fights broke out, and for the remainder of the year policemen patrolled the halls. That event changed me. I understood, from my own experience, the sacrifices the black students were forced to make. They had given up everything to go to a school whose culture bore no resemblance to their previous school's culture. I also witnessed young black men who were afraid to compete academically with white male students. The plight of people to survive is something I understood well.

Years later, after completing my doctorate and serving as deputy superintendent, I had the opportunity to invite Ruby Payne, who had just published *A Framework for Understanding Poverty*, to speak to my principals. I asked her if she had given any thought to how her work applied to gifted children from poverty. "No," she said, "but it certainly does, Paul. With your expertise, why don't you write about that?"

The result, two years later, was *Removing the Mask: Giftedness in Poverty*, coauthored by Ruby and me. It was also the beginning of my conducting trainings throughout the country on working with students from poverty and resulted in my writing *Hear Our Cry: Boys in Crisis*. Those experiences led Ruby and me to write the present book.

In the end, my difficult childhood, with all its rough spots, was a great gift. It gave me perseverance, a strong work ethic, and the ability to function amid chaos, qualities that have sustained me and propelled me forward. Relationships pay off. Education pays off. I know firsthand that boys coming from harsh beginnings can succeed.

—Paul Slocumb

Introduction

In any discipline, there are three stages of research: classification, correlation, and causation (Goldratt, 1999). We know of certain factors correlated with dropout—for example, the correlation between prison and male dropouts. This book goes a step beyond correlation and begins to examine the myriad causes behind the disengagement that leads to boys' dropping out, and how these causes are exacerbated by poverty.

A study conducted by the National Dropout Prevention Center describes dropping out as a process, not an event (Hammond, Linton, Smink, & Drew, 2007). Who are the students who go through this process?

- Nationally, about 70 percent of students graduate from high school on time with a regular diploma, but little more than half of African American and Hispanic students earn diplomas with their peers (Alliance for Excellent Education, 2009).*

- Approximately two thousand high schools (about 14 percent of American high schools) produce more than half of the nation's dropouts. In these dropout factories, the number of seniors enrolled is routinely 60 percent or less than the number of freshmen three years earlier. Dropout factories produce 81 percent of all Native American dropouts, 73 percent of all African American dropouts, and 66 percent of all Hispanic dropouts (Balfanz, 2007).

- More than one third of all dropouts occur in the ninth grade (Alliance for Excellent Education, 2009).

- Approximately 75 percent of state prison inmates did not complete high school (Harlow, 2003).

* The dropout statistics reported in this book are conservative numbers. Accuracy of dropout data is nebulous, because there is no standard dropout reporting system from state to state, and current systems in many states are manipulated because of accountability and political pressure. For example, a school district in 2009 of 75,000+ students reported a dropout number of five students. That number was determined by a system that allowed the district to not count as dropouts students who stated that they had moved to another school or were going to be home schooled. Insufficient follow-up of reported reasons contributes to data inaccuracies.

- A male high school graduate with a D average is fourteen times more likely to become incarcerated than a graduate with an A average (Arum & Beattie, 1999).

- A student coming from the highest quartile of family income is about seven times as likely to have completed high school as a student coming from the lowest quartile (Snyder, Dillow, & Hoffman, 2007).

Many of these dropouts cite a lack of connections to meaning or significant relationships (Bridgeland, Dilulio, & Morison, 2006). Other students drop out because of family pressures. For example, many males whose parents are unskilled immigrants leave school because the expectation is that they will work to help support the family. Compounding the problem for immigrant families are language issues and the sense of not belonging.

Situational and Generational Poverty

The amount of financial resources that the Child Welfare Fund defines as extreme poverty is half that cited by the federal government. By this account, more than 1 in 6—13.3 million—children in the United States are poor. The federal poverty line for a family of four in 2008 was $21,200. A family of four was *extremely* poor in 2008 if its household income was below $10,600 a year. There is, however, great variation in poverty rates for children among the states, ranging from a low of 1 in 12 in New Hampshire to a high of almost 3 in 10 in Mississippi (U.S. Census Bureau, 2010). Males, especially, suffer in poverty, because poverty around the world tends to be feminized. War, lack of work, crime, and drugs create instability, and often the women are left to care for the children alone.

There is an important distinction to be made between *situational* and *generational* poverty. Situational poverty develops when there is death, divorce, or illness, and the resource base is temporarily reduced. Generational poverty is when the family has been in poverty for two generations or more. Because of the intergenerational transfer of knowledge and the instability of resources, children in generational poverty do not develop in the same ways as children in more stable, knowledgeable environments (Najman et al., 2004; Payne, 2005). When the poverty spans generations, problems are magnified.

Why Should We Care?

Why is there such concern about dropout? In addition to the obvious moral issue of millions of young people not living up to their potential, there is an economic concern: the cost to society is huge.

- Dropouts from the class of 2007 alone cost the nation nearly $329 billion in lost wages, taxes, and productivity over their lifetimes (Education Commission of the States, 2007).

- Approximately 75 percent of state prison inmates did not complete high school (Harlow, 2003).

- American businesses currently spend more than $60 billion each year on training, much of that total on remedial reading, writing, and mathematics (Alliance for Excellent Education, 2003b).

- Over the course of a lifetime, a high school dropout in the United States earns, on average, about $260,000 less than a high school graduate (Rouse, 2005).

- The United States military no longer accepts high school dropouts, not even those who have earned a GED (General Education Diploma). "The Army is not accepting people with a GED in most areas of the country," reports its website, but "the Army reserves the right to waive certain disqualifications and allow enlistment if deemed in the best interest of the individual and the service" (U.S. Army Info Site, 2009). Less than 10 percent of recruits for the army, navy, and air force are accepted with a GED.

A dropout-related cost that often doesn't get calculated is the cost to districts in lost revenue. The Worksheet to Calculate Cost of Dropouts in the appendix (page 98) will show you how to cost this out. The worksheet identifies four multipliers: (1) the cost of the loss of daily attendance money, (2) the cost of a student repeating a course, (3) the cost of personnel time, and (4) the cost of alternative education settings. In the example provided, the annual cost to a district with one thousand students per class having a 60 percent graduation rate (close to the national average) would be $9,570,000.

Red-Flag Behaviors

To be sure, not all high-risk students drop out of high school. Most are resilient and find ways to beat the odds. But a number of factors—poor teachers, bullies, neighborhood problems, and family or personal issues—can lead to the following behaviors, which Heatherly Conway (2006) has identified as indicators that students are at risk of dropping out:

- Truancy, or missed days of school for family reasons

- Patterns of tardiness

- "Acting out" or withdrawn behaviors

- Knowledge of, or conversation about, sex and drugs that seems inappropriate for the child's age or stage of development
- Delays in common adaptive-behavior skills
- Lower-than-expected academic performance
- Inability to build or maintain appropriate peer or adult relationships
- Anxiety, fearfulness, flinching
- Inability to cope with transitions during the school day
- Lethargy; sleeping at school
- Hunger
- Poor hygiene
- Encopresis, enuresis, or unusual toileting habits
- Unusual eating patterns or habits
- Somatic complaints
- Moving frequently from school to school

In the ensuing chapters, we identify ways to keep the engagement process high for boys, beginning in elementary school, by providing specific resources and support for boys at risk of dropping out. It is our hope that with greater awareness, educators will take more steps to keep boys who come from poverty in school. It is heartbreaking to see the loss of incredible talent that results from conflict between the needs of the system and the needs of the student. To achieve optimum results, educators and communities must address these engagement issues early. Our success in doing so will not only have a positive impact on our society but will also promote its sustainability.

1

The Impact of Generational Poverty on Boys

Prior to the 1980s, most researchers believed that biology was destiny. Then, a number of researchers came to the conclusion that the opposite was true: it was the way a child is raised, rather than the child's biology, that determined behavior—*nurture* rather than *nature*. The relatively recent advent of neuroscience has advanced the nature argument a great deal, and brain scans have shown marked differences in the physiological structures of the male and female brain. Michael Gurian (2006), in *The Wonder of Boys*, sums up our current knowledge as follows: "It's more accurate to say that much of who we are is determined by body chemicals, brain differences, hormones, and by society's efforts to honor this biology through its socializing influences" (p. 5).

In this book, we map out the way biology—nature—affects the ways boys behave and learn, and creates their unique emotional and disciplinary needs. We do this in order to show educators how their interactions with boys— nurture—can best help them reach their potential. We agree with the following argument of Gurian (2006):

> Because biology is proclivity, when our children are young, we must do everything we can to help boys and girls feel comfortable in the development of their own separate ways of doing things. Not to do so is to teach them that their core self is inadequate by nature and will not be nurtured by society. Our children, brought up this way, will take their revenge. (p. 13)

The following cautionary tale is about the journey of one boy who was *not* nurtured by family, school, or society—and dropped out of school. The names have been changed, but the story is true.

Devin's Story

Devin was born to Kathy and Joe. Kathy had lost custody of another child in a previous divorce settlement, and Joe had a son, Seth, from his first marriage, who lived with his mother. Born in late August, Devin was handsome, with an easygoing disposition. Both Joe and Kathy used marijuana and drank. When Joe drank, he often became violent. Kathy had been so happy to be pregnant that she saw a doctor during the pregnancy and stopped drinking and smoking marijuana. She resumed using both soon after Devin was born.

When Devin was two, Joe and Kathy moved to a low-income neighborhood in a small Midwestern town five blocks away from Seth and his mother. It was not unusual, in this neighborhood, for the police to answer domestic violence calls.

Kathy was smart and had a high school diploma, as did Joe. She worked hourly wage jobs in a factory, but was there for Devin emotionally. Joe worked in trailer factories and was sometimes absent—particularly when he was running from the law. Devin was the only child in the household, but Seth would sometimes come over on weekends. Not long after Devin started to talk, it became obvious he had a stuttering problem. Joe was merciless in making fun of Devin's stutter and would yell at him to stop. Whenever his dad made fun of him, Devin would just laugh.

Devin went to a neighborhood elementary school within walking distance. The school provided a speech pathologist to work with Devin, but his stuttering didn't improve. He was an average student, not strong in reading or math, but he didn't fail either. He was likable, not mean-spirited, and had a lot of friends. After school, he would often go to the nearby Boys & Girls Club, because both his parents were at work. He liked sports and played them during and after school. He played football, and really liked the coach, who encouraged him.

Devin and his mother were close, and because he was large for his age, he sometimes protected her from his father's periodic violence and abuse. Devin would occasionally skip school and not finish his homework, and the school had to call more than once.

In seventh grade, Devin dropped out of sports. He was also having difficulty in math. His mother told the guidance counselor that she was never good in math, so it wasn't realistic to expect Devin to be, but she said she would talk to him about it. That year Devin got into a couple of fights with students who made fun of his stuttering.

In eighth grade, he failed math and language arts. That year, Kathy went back to community college to become a nurse. She had to take several remedial classes, and Joe was so upset that she was going back to school that he became more abusive, was temporarily jailed, and ran to another state to avoid being arrested again. He was gone for about five months.

Devin's attendance was worse, but Kathy confided in a friend, "How can I ask him to go to school when he's such a help to me when Joe gets violent?" Devin went to summer school to try and make up the credits.

In tenth grade, the patterns continued. He didn't go to summer school. In eleventh grade, Devin dropped out.

Teachers' Perceptions of Devin

What follows are comments about Devin from teachers, administrators, counselors, and his coach.*

Sixth Grade

- Mrs. M., science teacher: "Charming sense of humor. But he's lazy. Not devoted to school. Sometimes very distracted. May be ADHD."

- Mr. J., math teacher: "Devin has no sense of money or math. Has many friends but no real motivation to do well."

- Mr. G., football coach: "Incredible potential in football. Big for his age and a good linebacker. Have worked with him to get him to come to school and practice every day, and for the most part, he does. Other players really like him. Stuttering is an issue."

- Mr. B., assistant principal: "Kept Devin in for detention for his tardies and absences. He is good-natured and doesn't seem to mind being there, but he hasn't changed his patterns."

- Mrs. K., counselor: "Talked to Devin's mother about his absences, and she said she would try to do better. She said it was hard to wake him up in the morning. He stayed up late watching TV."

Seventh Grade

- Mrs. D., administrator: "Fight started over an eighth-grader mimicking Devin's stutter. Devin hit him and broke his nose. Suspended Devin for a week."

---

*A note about the negativity of the staff is in order. These comments do not come from an actual taped meeting and were not made in a professional setting. They were relayed to us by the individual who was involved with Devin's case.

- Mr. G., football coach: "Devin dropped out of football today. Stated he just couldn't make all the practices and that he was failing courses and would be dropped anyway. Needed to be at home for his mother. But his friends say he is at the Boys & Girls Club until nine o'clock at night. Not sure what is going on there."
- Mrs. M., science teacher: "Doesn't do homework. Laughs about it when I reprimand him in front of the class, then he tells a joke about stuttering. Basically he wastes my time. Called his mother, and that was a waste of time, too. Looks like a dropout in the making."

Eighth Grade

- Ms. R., counselor: "He has failed language arts and math the last two years, but we've decided to place Devin in ninth grade. He's big for his age and needs to be moved on."

Ninth Grade

- Mr. W., algebra teacher: "Another example of middle-school teachers being worthless. Why do they pass these kids on to high school? It makes me crazy. If you don't know that 9 times 9 is 81, how in the hell are you going to be able to handle algebra? I'm no babysitter."
- Mr. H., industrial arts teacher: "I really enjoy Devin. He's teachable, easy to get along with, has a great sense of humor and rapport with other students, and enjoys working with his hands. I talked to him about attendance, and I've noticed that lately he has been coming more regularly."
- Mrs. S., language arts/English teacher: "His stuttering is so bad that I haven't asked him to do a speech in front of the class. And his writing is so poor. Not sure what to do with him. This is my first year as a teacher, and Devin doesn't cause trouble in class, so I just leave him alone."
- Mr. P., counselor: "I called Devin in today, introduced myself, and explained that he had failed two classes—algebra, English—and that he would need to take summer school and pay for it. He said he could do that. He was very pleasant. I do worry about his stuttering, though."

Tenth Grade

- Mrs. C., counselor: "I called Devin's mother and explained that he had failed algebra I in summer school and so would need to repeat it. She laughed and said she had never been any good in math, either. I also commented on his attendance. The mother told me she wasn't going to say anything to Devin about his attendance because he protected her when his father got violent."

- Mr. W., algebra I teacher: "They put that idiot Devin back in my class again for another round of algebra I. What am I? A magician?"

- Mr. L., administrator: "Look at the part of town that boy is from. It's a miracle he's as decent as he is. What do you expect? I called him in the other day about his attendance and said I was going to call his dad. He just laughed and told me good luck—his dad was hiding from the cops right now in some other state—and if I could find out where he was, to 'let me know.' There's nothing the school can do for a kid like that. He's wasting our time."

Eleventh Grade

Devin comes in for the first month of school and then drops out.

Reflections on Devin's Story

Is Devin typical of boys who drop out of high school? Yes and no. Every story, to be sure, is unique, but there are many factors and forces in Devin's life that are found across the board among at-risk students, particularly those who are male and come from poverty. Could more have been done by educators to help him succeed? Absolutely. Did these educators have a tough task on their hands? Absolutely. So, we need to ask ourselves, do students like Devin simply drop out—or are they pushed out? The answer is both.

Teaching is a highly complex task that takes a great deal of energy and requires educators to access multiple types of information simultaneously. Coupled with this is the fact that to teach well, a teacher needs data—not just about a class, but about each individual student. At the secondary level, it is not unusual for a teacher to have 150 students. To sort all that input faster, the brain patterns information. One strategy teachers use, for the sake of simple survival, is to write off students whose issues are too complex to address or who are perceived as taking too much energy. Sometimes, too, in the process of patterning information, the student himself is seen as a pattern rather than a person. Because of time constraints, demands of teaching, fatigue, or lack of awareness, the inquiry necessary to investigate the details behind that pattern is not done.

Communities in Schools collaborated with the National Dropout Prevention Center at Clemson University to conduct a comprehensive study of dropouts in the United States (Hammond et al., 2007). After reviewing the literature from a wide range of sources spanning twenty-five years (1980–2005), they identified risk categories and risk factors for dropout. Table 1.1 shows the result.

Table 1.1: Significant Risk Categories and Factors by School Level

Key: √ indicates that the risk factor was found   √* indicates that the risk factor was found
          to be significantly related to dropout at   to be significantly related to dropout at
          this school level in one study.   this school level in two or more studies.

Risk Category / Risk Factor	Elementary School	Middle School	High School
Individual Background Characteristics			
Learning disability or emotional disturbance		√	√
Early Adult Responsibilities			
High number of work hours		√	√*
Parenthood			√*
Social Attitudes, Values, & Behavior			
High-risk peer group		√*	√
High-risk social behavior		√*	√
Highly socially active outside of school			√
School Performance			
Low achievement	√*	√*	√*
Retention/over age for grade	√*	√*	√*
School Engagement			
Poor attendance	√*	√*	√*

Risk Category / Risk Factor	Elementary School	Middle School	High School
Low educational expectations		√*	√*
Lack of effort		√	√
Low commitment to school		√	√*
Lack of extracurricular participation		√	√*
School Behavior			
Misbehavior	√	√	√*
Early aggression	√	√	
Family Background Characteristics			
Low socioeconomic status	√*	√*	√*
High family mobility		√*	
Low educational level of parents	√	√	√*
Large number of siblings	√		√
Not living with both natural parents	√	√	√*
Family disruption	√		
Family Engagement/Commitment to Education			
Low educational expectations		√*	
Sibling dropped out		√	√
Low contact with school		√*	
Lack of conversations about school		√*	√

Reprinted with permission of the National Dropout Prevention Center and Communities in Schools.

Beginning school and then dropping out is analogous to beginning and ending a personal relationship. No one enters school thinking, "When will I drop out?" any more than a couple enter a marriage thinking, "When will we divorce?" Just as relationships become increasingly complex as families come together, children are born, careers are built, homes are purchased and sold, jobs are lost, careers take a new turn, illness strikes, and moves are made to new surroundings, so school becomes increasingly complex for students as content and processes become more difficult, consequences for behavior become more severe, more and more teachers interact with the student, interests outside of school compete with schoolwork, and families and teachers interact, agree, and disagree. To continue the analogy, when a personal relationship takes a downward turn, it is not usually due to one specific event, though one event may provide the spark. So it is with school; a variety of factors contribute to students' dropping out.

Risk Factors and Interventions

Using table 1.1, let's look at Devin's risk factors and the types of interventions that might have prevented him from dropping out of school.

- **Learning disability**—Although he received speech therapy in school, it was not effective. Devin was entitled to service prior to kindergarten, and early intervention is critical with language problems. His parents did not avail themselves of this service.

- **High-risk peer group**—A counselor working with Devin might have been able to detect the violence that surrounded Devin's world and connect the family with social services.

- **Low achievement**—Devin was younger than his classmates, and his stuttering interfered with his learning. Devin needed a tutor and more time to complete assignments. Without support at home, he needed to find support within the school in the form of adults who made sure he attended summer school, helped him transition from fiction to nonfiction reading (second to third grade), encouraged real-world application of math (for example, measuring the classroom, measuring space, and dividing food to learn fractions), presented real-world application of algebra (using cell phone bills, car payments, and interest multipliers), used mental models, and made sure he had a future story. (See the Future Story exercise in the appendix, page 109.)

- **Retention or over age for grade**—Because he was younger than his classmates, and because he had a learning disability, the probability that he would have difficulty socializing with others was greatly increased. Ongoing counseling might have helped Devin with this difficulty. Putting Devin in a transitional first grade may have helped with his delay in reading and language development.

- **Poor attendance**—Devin desperately needed to connect with someone at the school. Sports seemed to be an incentive for him to attend school and bring up his grades. If the coach had implemented a tutorial program for Devin, he probably would have been more effective in getting Devin to school.

- **Low educational expectations**—Because Devin's parents did not have high expectations for him academically, someone from the school needed to connect with Devin and build a significant, meaningful relationship with him. Students will frequently work to please a respected, caring adult.

- **Lack of effort**—Summer school was not enough for Devin to get caught up academically. He could have benefited from a homework hour offered before school began. The Honor Society students provide help for students like Devin as part of their service hours. His homework assignments should also have had actual value, as opposed to being perceived as busy work.

- **Low commitment to school**—Devin's low commitment to school was aggravated by his teachers' negative attitudes about him, which were probably communicated both overtly and covertly. Here, again, a meaningful relationship with a caring adult could have made a significant difference in Devin's schooling.

- **No extracurricular participation**—Because Devin loved sports, the school missed an important opportunity to help him. The coaches could have been a key support system.

- **Misbehavior**—Devin was not a discipline problem. No intervention was needed.

- **Early aggression**—Devin was not an aggressive child. In fact, he was well liked. No intervention was necessary.

- **Low socioeconomic status**—Devin came from a poor household and lived in a poor neighborhood. The school could not change the economic status of the family; however, it could have regarded it as a warning sign that Devin would need extra support in school.

- **High family mobility**—Devin's family did not move frequently. Once they moved to the Midwest, they stayed. No intervention was needed.

- **Low educational level of parents**—Though both parents graduated from high school, they were not strong students, and their lack of performance in school affected their expectations for Devin, which were similarly low. School personnel could have spent more time counseling Devin's parents, especially his mother, about his potential.

- **Large number of siblings**—Devin was an only child. He had occasional contact with his half brother. No intervention was needed.

- **Not living with both parents**—Social services needed to be informed of the domestic violence and his father's periodic absences due to criminal activity.

- **Family disruption**—Domestic violence was frequent, and drugs and alcohol were abused in the family. The approach taken by a high school in Colorado could have been used with Devin. There, the school provided support groups facilitated by a counselor for students with complex issues. One support group was for rape and sexual abuse, one for families with substance abuse issues, and one for students with family members who were seriously ill or dying.

- **Sibling has dropped out**—Devin had no siblings; however, his half-brother Seth dropped out of school at sixteen. When a student's friends or siblings are not performing well academically and are dropping out of school, that student is more likely to drop out (Hammond et al., 2007). Devin needed help in forming relationships with students who saw school and academics as a positive experience.

- **Low contact with school**—Making home visits might have helped Devin's parents, especially his mother, be more supportive of school. By making a ten-minute video about their content, classroom, and subject matter, burning it to a CD, and sending it home, teachers might have involved her more. They might also have sent text messages to her cell phone detailing specific homework assignments or issues.

- **Lack of conversations about school**—Making home visits and encouraging his mother to attend some parenting classes might have helped Devin, especially in the earlier grades.

The Need for Early Intervention

The more early warning signs and risk factors a boy demonstrates, the greater the need for early intervention to prevent a future dropout. Typically, schools use supplemental funds for programs in the upper elementary grades (additional tutoring, after-school programs, summer programs) to help students catch up. And because states do competency testing in reading, writing, and math in the upper elementary grades, these remediation efforts are in reaction to high-stakes testing. However, a more efficient use of money is to allocate funds to the early primary grades to prevent initial failure. Such interventions may require more personnel, parent conferences, and home visits, as well the assistance of specialists and social services or other outside agencies.

Title I Funds

Title I funds are commonly thought of as targeting high-poverty schools. In a PowerPoint presentation on the *National Assessment of Title I: Interim Report to Congress* (Pendleton & Stullich, 2008), the authors note, "In the highest poverty schools, Title I funding per low-income student has not changed since 1997–98, after adjusting for inflation." In addition, they noted, "high-poverty schools continue to receive less funding per low-income student than low-poverty schools." Published figures from school year 2003–04 show that 32 percent of Title I participants were in grades 1 through 3, while 28 percent were in grades 4 through 6 (Dabney, 2007). While most Title I dollars are spent at the elementary level, these funds are generally used to support staff rather than programs or curricula (Chambers et al., 2009). Primary-grade intervention is crucial in reducing the dropout rate. Why wait until the child has failed in his struggle to read and write?

Early Assessment

Students who lag behind in reading, writing, and math in the first two months of school should be placed in tutorials, as well as before- and after-school programs, to avoid the need to remediate in the upper grades. To determine which students will need extra support, do a kindergarten roundup in April and May and give those children a readiness test or tests. Place those who don't have the requisite skills in a summer program that includes intensive oral language development, gross and fine motor skills development, and phonemic awareness. Students who were enrolled in a prekindergarten program should automatically be included in the summer program, as should students from Head Start programs.

Assess the resources available to students in kindergarten through twelfth grade in the following areas:

- **Financial resources**—Does the family have the money to purchase goods and services?

- **Language resources**—Is the student able to speak and use formal register in writing and in speech?

- **Emotional resources**—Is the student able to choose and control emotional responses, particularly to negative situations, without engaging in self-destructive behavior?

- **Mental resources**—Does the student have the cognitive abilities and acquired skills (reading, writing, computing) to deal with daily life?

- **Spiritual resources**—Does the student believe his life has a meaning and purpose? Does he have optimism and hope?

- **Physical resources**—Does the student possess physical health and mobility?

- **Support systems**—Does the student have external resources— friends, family, and backup resources—available in times of need?

- **Relationships and role models**—Does the student have frequent access to adult(s) who are appropriate and nurturing and who do not engage in self-destructive behavior?

- **Knowledge of hidden rules**—Does the student know the unspoken cues and habits of a group?

From the beginning, parents need to be included. When parents are remiss in getting their children to school in the early grades, be very firm with them. Parents, like Devin's mom, need to know early in their child's academic career that educators are serious about children being in school. Students and parents who think it's okay to arrive late or miss school in the elementary grades won't think it's important at the secondary level, either. Bad habits that develop early are hard to break. As much as possible, teachers must work to prevent them from forming in the first place.

Brain development and cognitive development are at their peak from birth to ten years of age (Sousa, 2001). If the foundation created during those years is strong, it will minimize problems at the secondary level. In the long run, it's also much cheaper to intervene at the elementary than the secondary level. Young children are eager to learn, but the more they struggle and experience failure, the less likely they are to enjoy learning. The challenge for everyone who works with at-risk students is to do everything possible to help them succeed, to minimize the barriers they face and maximize the building blocks of success.

2

The Physical Development
of Boys

In this chapter, we look at developmental differences between boys and girls and at how these differences affect learning. We explore the impact of generational poverty on boys' physical development and learning and provide strategies to both support that development and prevent dropout.

Motor Skills

Male and female fetuses look the same during the first six weeks of life, and then things change dramatically. Around the sixth week, the Y chromosome triggers the development of the testes, which secrete testosterone. This hormone has a significant impact on the development of the brain and, together with other hormones, contributes to a very different developmental trajectory for boys (Baron-Cohen, Lutchmaya, & Knickmeyer, 2004).

In *Boys Adrift*, Leonard Sax (2007) writes that among the most striking findings of research has been the discovery that "the various regions of the brain develop in a different sequence and tempo in girls compared with boys" (p. 17). In boys, for example, gross motor skills develop at a much faster rate than do fine motor skills (Berk, 1997; Cohen, 1997; Cole & Cole, 1993; Poest, Williams, Witt, & Atwood, 1989). Gross motor skills involve the large muscles of the body and are used in such activities as walking, running, lifting, sitting, and throwing. Fine motor skills are the small, refined movements of the hands, fingers, and thumbs required to button a shirt, draw, or write. The delayed development of fine motor skills can lead to a boy's dislike for any schoolwork that requires attention to detail. Writing in *Newsweek*, Peg Tyre (2006) said that boys

> bring to kindergarten a set of physical and mental abilities very different from girls. . . . Boys tend to have better hand-eye coordination, but their fine motor skills are less developed, making it a struggle for some to control a pencil or a paintbrush. Boys are more impulsive than girls; even if they can sit still, many prefer not to—at least not for long.

A Harvard University study concurs: "By school age, the average boy in a classroom is more active than the girls—even the most active girls don't seem to express their energy in the unrestrained way characteristic of most boys" (PBS Parents, n.d.).

In *Boy Writers*, Ralph Fletcher (2006) finds that boys' fine motor skills lag behind girls' as late as fifth grade. Fletcher cites a fifth-grade teacher's comment that "the first . . . thing I notice is that boys have a harder time writing neatly and quickly" (p. 73). This early aversion to writing tends to escalate in adolescence, when teachers require more and more paper activities.

Spatial Ability

Spatial ability means "the perceptions of the relationships of objects that determine our understanding of place" (Nabhan & Trimble, 1994, p. 184). It allows one to "picture in one's mind the shape of things, their dimensions, coordinates, proportions, movement, and geography" (Pease & Pease, 2000, p. 102). Males' exposure to higher levels of testosterone before birth gives them an added advantage with regard to spatial ability, a gap that continues into adulthood (Cole, 2007). Moore and Frost, quoted in Gurian's *The Wonder of Boys* (2006), state:

> During fetal life, when the brain and nervous system are being organized, the female cortex (brain) develops in advance of the male cortex. The left half of the cortex (the part of the brain that controls thinking) develops somewhat later than the right (the part that works with spatial relationships). In males, though, there is an even greater lag. "As a result," one neurologist says, "when the right side is ready to hook up with the left side (by sending over connecting nerve fibers), in the male the appropriate cells don't yet exist on the left. So (the fibers) go back and instead form connections within the right hemisphere. You end up with extremely enriched connections within the right." (p. 13)

It is not surprising that, as young children, boys tend to prefer mechanical toys and games (Allen, 2000; Ben-Chaim, Lappan, & Houang, 1988; Kolb & Whishaw, 2008).

Differences in the perception of space also affect the way boys process their emotional needs. Males need more room in which to deal with their feelings. When emotions hit, boys have to "go away" to process them (Slocumb, 2007). William Pollack (1998) calls this the "timed silence syndrome" (p. 8). Boys not only need more space to process their emotions, they need more time in which to do it.

Environmental Factors

Toxins in the environment have a direct effect on boys' physical development. Endocrine disruptors found in herbicides, pesticides, fertilizers, and plastics alter the way human hormones work and can even influence the male sperm count (Gurian, 1999). According to ecotoxicologists Martin Wagner and Jörg Oehlmann (2009) at Goethe University in Germany, the now ubiquitous plastic water bottles contaminate the water contained in them with these estrogenic chemicals. Sax (2007) writes that one effect of the chemicals used in manufacturing plastic is to cause an increase in estrogen and a decrease in testosterone, creating more brittle bones and a decreased sex drive in boys.

A result, according to a study by the *International Journal of Impotence* (Medical News, 2004), is that more and more young men are turning to Viagra for recreational use, and this drug has become an increasingly requested drug on college campuses. Also popular are Ritalin and similar drugs, such as Concerta, Metadate, Dexedrine, and Adderall, which increase focus and concentration.

Researchers for the pharmaceutical industry report that in a study of more than 5 million adult males between the ages of eighteen and forty-five increased their use of Viagra by 312 percent, and those between the ages of forty-six to fifty-five increased their use by 216 percent over the study period (Medical News, 2004). An anonymous survey of 234 sexually active male students at three college campuses conducted by researchers at Children's Memorial Hospital found that 6 percent have used erectile-dysfunction medications. Many of these young men combined male enhancement drugs with alcohol, which can affect blood pressure as well as the exercise of discrimination in the choice of sexual partners (Springen, 2006).

Adolescent Growth

Adolescence occurs later for most boys than it does girls. Girls may begin puberty as young as nine or ten, while for boys it tends to occur around the ages of eleven or twelve, when they experience growth spurts due to the elevation of testosterone in their bloodstream (Baron-Cohen, Lutchmaya, & Knickmeyer, 2004). An average boy's production of testosterone increases tenfold during this period (British Broadcasting Company, n.d.). Eventually, boys will have about twenty times as much testosterone as girls (Baron-Cohen, Lutchmaya, & Knickmeyer, 2004). In four years, the average teenage boy will grow a foot taller, put on twenty pounds of muscle, drop an octave in the pitch of his voice, and develop 40 percent more heart muscle. He will also acquire body and facial hair and develop body odor (British Broadcasting Company, n.d.).

During this time, boys continue to need more space for movement and for emotional processing. This becomes problematic when schools try to force boys to fit the environment, rather than make changes in the environment that will accommodate boys' needs during this period of dramatic physical change.

Mood Swings

Teenage boys experience mood swings due to hormone fluctuations that can occur daily. These hormone fluctuations may be high in the morning, drop midday, and rise again later in the day. Any rapid fluctuation in hormones is usually accompanied by irritability, recklessness, aggression, and depression (British Broadcasting Corporation, n.d.). Unlike boys, girls tend to experience their mood swings monthly.

Sax (2007) points to two educational trends, in particular, that fail to take into account boys' adolescent mood swings: changes in the way physical education is taught and "zero tolerance" policies regarding violence. Ironically, zero tolerance for violence sometimes results in a lack of acceptance of boys even writing or talking about violence, thus depriving them of an important outlet for their natural aggression.

The spiking of testosterone may also increase a boy's competitiveness. Competition engages most boys because they are competitive by nature; boys who aren't into physical sports may spend more time playing video games to meet this competitive need. Sax (2007) argues that loss in competition is part of the reason boys disengage from school.

Boys also experience *rest states* periodically. Rest states are when the brain literally shuts down (Gurian & Henley, 2001). Boys generally want people to get to the point. They are "bullet thinkers" and tend to get lost in the words.

When boys are bombarded with lengthy explanations, they tend to disengage and go into a rest state. One mother shared with us that once, when she was telling her ten-year-old son something, he looked up at her and said, "Mom, is this going to take long?" In the classroom, the rest state often appears as the glazed-over look we take to be daydreaming. Boys sometimes tap pencils as a way of avoiding the rest state—which may get them in trouble, or elicit a comment like "You're not paying attention." Having a place in the classroom where a boy can move around or giving him a squeeze ball to play with can help him stay out of his rest state. Other strategies that help prevent the rest state are moving closer to the boy, asking him a question, or having him physically do something. Making the activity into a game that appeals to his competitiveness also helps avoid the rest state.

Roughhousing

Boys need movement. It is daunting for some boys to come into the classroom, sit down, and get to work. For those boys, school becomes a prison. Changing classes during the school day helps, but often that isn't enough. This need for movement is also apparent in the way boys roughhouse with other boys, an important developmental step through which boys learn to find the line between aggression and violence.

Recent studies show that children whose fathers play in a rough-and-tumble way with them as toddlers are rated as more popular and less aggressive than their peers (Durham, 2003). Play fighting provides dads with a powerful way of teaching their sons the physical self-control they'll need later as boyfriends, partners, and fathers themselves (Biddulph, 1998; Pollack, 1998). These activities give young boys a socially acceptable form of physical touch and closeness. Psychologist Kate Klein (n.d.) writes:

> One could argue that the reason most children do not develop problems with aggression is because they are presented with opportunities to experience intense negative emotions as infants, engage in aggression as toddlers, and are discouraged in various ways from repeating unacceptable behavior.

During adolescence, this roughhousing turns to horseplay, with boys poking and slapping one another, as well as jumping up and touching the door frame or ceiling. Poking, shoving, and slapping are ways boys communicate affection toward other boys, but horseplay can also get them in trouble in school and may cross a line, triggering anger and resulting in fighting (Pitcher & Schultz, 1983; Weiss, 1991). For many boys, the fighting becomes a sign of prowess and a badge of honor, often increasing their status in the eyes of other boys (Jordan, 1995; Kimmel, 2000).

Generational Poverty and Boys' Physical Development

Generational poverty magnifies issues associated with the physical development of boys in the following ways:

- **Inadequate diet**—The United Nations defines wealth throughout the world based, in part, on whether you have protein in your diet on a daily basis (UNICEF, 2007). Because protein tends to be a more expensive form of food, the diet of those in poverty tends to be high in carbohydrates and fats. Carbohydrates help the brain make serotonin, and serotonin helps keep you from being depressed. Carbohydrates therefore become an inexpensive antidepressant.

  People in poverty also have less access to fresh vegetables and fruits. Without nutrients in the bloodstream, learning is a much more difficult endeavor. Other dietary issues have also been linked to poverty. If your family moves a lot, you may not have pots and pans with which to cook. If your electricity gets cut off, you don't have access to an oven or stove or microwave. In poverty around the world, food is typically eaten with hands and not utensils. This makes the consumption of food less sanitary. If your food comes from an area with high amounts of environmental toxins in the air, water, and ground, then the food also has toxins.

- **Sexual illiteracy**—Particularly for adolescents living in poverty, the changing body is a source of amusement and teasing and sometimes the object of hazing. Wet dreams, unexpected sexual reactions and responses, changing voices, growth spurts, aching legs and knees, and the growth of facial and pubic hair are rarely explained. Tools for dealing with the issues are seldom provided, beyond what is covered in the occasional health class. Boys without fathers are left to wander through this maze alone. Other adult males are usually unavailable to respond to questions. The primary sources of information are same-age peers, the Internet, and television.

- **Unhealthy living conditions**—Medical and dental care, vitamins, places to exercise and play, cleanliness, healthy sexual boundaries, and living space are often in short supply in poverty. Environmental toxins that pollute the air, such as fertilizers, fuel emissions, pollen, and so on, can also limit or prevent physical activity (Berliner, 2009). Organically grown foods are not on the shelves of the local convenience store on the corner, and even if they are obtainable, tend to be more expensive. The mind may also be left undernourished in poverty. In educated households, parents buy toys, puzzles, and objects for children to manipulate that develop visual, auditory, and motor skills. They send their children to summer camp and enroll them in summer activities. Most of these resources simply are not available in poverty.

- **Lack of safety**—Violence is a given in many poor neighborhoods, and the possibility of early death is a nearly constant companion. In the United States, in the five years prior to 2008, thirty thousand people died in gun violence (U.S. Conference of Mayors, 2008). Most of the victims were from poverty. In a study published in 2009, 15 percent of adolescents, a greater number of whom were minority or low income, believed they would die before they were thirty (Berliner, 2009). In extreme urban-poverty neighborhoods, many parents don't even let their children outside because of drive-by shootings, gang wars, and drug-related violence. As a result, even a physiological resource as basic as motor coordination may be lacking, despite boys' built-in advantage in this area. Sax (2005) writes: "If we fail to provide boys with pro-social models of the transition to adulthood, they may construct their own. In some cases, gang initiation rituals, street racing, and random violence may be the result" (p. 168). We explore this topic further in chapter 5, "The Social Development of Boys" (page 51).

Supporting the Physical Development of Boys

Table 2.1 (page 24) lists strategies schools can use to support boys' physical development, make school work for them, and prevent dropout.

Table 2.1: Supporting Boys' Physical Development to Prevent Dropout

Preschool Years (birth to age 4)	Provide breakfast and lunch.
	Work with churches and other community outreach organizations to disseminate information about the importance of nutrition.
	Teach personal hygiene.
Boyhood (ages 5–10, kindergarten –grade 5)	Use cooking as a way to teach math.
	Have after-school cooking classes.
	Provide breakfast and lunch.
	Provide karate or a similar discipline.
	Have the physical education curriculum focus on lifelong wellness and motor development, not just competitive athletics.
	Teach personal hygiene.
	Provide free, after-school tutorial and recreational programs in order to strengthen academic performance in a safe environment.
Adolescence (ages 11–16, grades 6–10)	Reinstate home and family arts (including cooking) classes in school.
	In biology classes, tie food and nutrition to an understanding of bodily systems.
	Have the physical education curriculum focus on lifelong wellness—not just competitive athletics.
	Teach students about sexually transmitted diseases. Many boys become sexually active during adolescence.
	Identify the ways in which food, drugs, alcohol, and cigarettes have an impact on physical wellness.
	Provide after-school programs, including tutorials and structured activities, in a safe environment.
Early Manhood (ages 17–23, grade 11 to post–high school)	Have each person identify the activities that he will use to stay physically fit.
	Identify the ways in which food, drugs, alcohol, and cigarettes have an impact on physical wellness.

3

The Emotional Development of Boys

In this chapter, we look at how boys' emotional development differs from that of girls, the significant role that anger and shame play in boys' lives and the relationship of these feelings to risk taking, and the effects of childhood abuse and trauma on boys' emotional development. We also discuss the effects these factors have on learning, how those effects are exacerbated by generational poverty, and what can be done to support the emotional development of boys in order to help them stay in school.

Brain Physiology and Boys' Emotions

The brain is a feeling machine that thinks, not a thinking machine that feels. Whatever goes into the brain goes in at a sensory level (Damasio, 1996, 2000; LeDoux, 1996; Llinas & Churchland, 1996). Every parent has experienced the frustration that comes with trying to guess what sensations an infant's cries and smiles are trying to communicate. A child who has acquired language and can say, "I'm thirsty," no longer has to cry to express a need, but because the transition from feelings to words occurs so quickly, we often fail to realize that these expressed needs are still being driven by the senses (Morose, 2006).

However, processing emotional information is much more difficult for boys of all ages than it is for girls. Some of this disparity is linked to biology. Though in males emotions are lodged in the amygdala, located deep in the medial temporal lobes, they are processed in the cerebral cortex, located at the front of the brain. In females, emotions are lodged in every part of the brain, and so travel a shorter distance for processing (Gurian, 2006; Neu & Weinfeld,

2007). As a result of both wiring and conditioning, boys need more time to process emotional information than girls. States Gurian (2006):

> As the male and female brains mature in the first decade of life, then through the hormonal adjustments of puberty, we see boys getting less and less able to connect feeling and verbal information in comparison to girls. (p. 23)

The male brain is hard-wired for doing, the female brain for talking. Studies in thirty-nine different countries bear this out (Halpern, 2000). When asked, "How do you think it made Bill feel when you did that?" a boy's response will typically be, "I don't know." And he doesn't! That is why, when boys are disciplined, they need *think time* to process the emotional information. Try to have a place in school where a boy who is being disciplined can sit quietly and process. Offer him a drink of water. Water helps to dilute cortisol (a stress hormone) secreted in the brain when a person gets angry or anxious. A rocking chair can also help a boy process his emotions, because it allows movement. When it is time to talk with the boy, take a walk around campus while conversing. A boy is much more likely to talk if he's also doing something else. Good counselors often have games in their offices: a boy will be more inclined to open up while playing a game or working a jigsaw puzzle (Gurian, 2006; Neu & Weinfeld, 2007; Pollack, 1998; Sax, 2005, 2007).

Gender Conditioning and Boys' Emotions

While some of boys' issues with emotions are hard wired, others are the result of gender conditioning—guys just don't talk about some things because it isn't cool (Jackson, 1990; Mahoney, 1985; Salisbury & Jackson, 1996). In fact, most boys shift from being emotionally reactive as babies to being virtually unresponsive as adolescents (Brody, 1996). Not talking about their emotions has consequences, because verbal expression improves impulse control. Dan Kindlon and Michael Thompson (2000) write, "This developmental lack of ease with verbal expression, combined with the cultural edict against talking about feelings, channels boys' emotional energy into action" (p. 43).

Emotional Literacy

Boys, in short, tend to be less emotionally literate than girls. Emotional literacy includes the ability to identify and name emotions, to recognize others' emotions, and to understand the situations or behaviors that cause emotions. Howard Gardner, in *Frames of Mind* (1993), explains the importance of feelings as follows:

> The less a person understands his own feelings, the more he will fall prey
> to them. The less a person understands the feelings, the responses, and
> the behavior of others, the more likely he will interact inappropriately with
> them and therefore fail to secure his proper place in the world. (p. 254)

Emotional expression, understanding, and regulation are crucial factors in competent social functioning (Denham, Mitchell-Copeland, Strandberg, Auerbach, & Blair, 1997; Saarni, 1999).

Because they lack the vocabulary and aren't nurtured to be in touch with their feelings in the ways most girls are—and because boys take longer to process their feelings than girls—when boys get emotionally aroused, they often don't manage these emotions very well and often express their emotions through anger and aggression (Kindlon & Thompson, 2000; Slocumb, 2007). The inability to manage emotions, in turn, affects their relationships with teachers and peers. It may also account for the fact that boys are four and a half times more likely than girls to be expelled from preschool (Gilliam, 2005).

One reason for boys' weaker emotional literacy is that mothers use a wider variety of "emotion words" with their daughters than they do with their sons—words such as *upset*, *crabby*, and *annoyed* rather than simply *sad*. Daniel Reisberg and Paula Hertel (2004) state:

> As children grow older, mothers talk increasingly of other people's emotions as well as the child's, especially with girls. Mothers also place emotions in a more social and relational context with girls than with boys. In reminiscing with daughters, mothers talk about how emotions emerge from, and are modulated by, interactions with other people, whereas with sons, they are more likely to discuss emotions as internal and autonomous experiences. These patterns suggest that mothers are providing a more embellished and differentiated understanding of emotion with daughters than with sons. . . . Further, by placing emotions in a more interpersonal context with daughters than with sons, parents may be teaching girls to integrate emotions into relationships with others to a greater extent than are boys. Thus, girls may be developing a more embellished, more differentiated, and more relational emotional self-concept than are boys. (pp. 246, 248)

Educators must help boys become emotionally literate and develop a feeling vocabulary—and this must be taught directly. In fact, most boys need a "Feeling-Word Thesaurus" (Slocumb, 2007). Ask students to create a non-linguistic representation for some feeling words, using pictures or cartoons

(Marzano, 2004). Use the following categories adapted from the work of Gloria Willcox (n.d.) as a springboard, and add more.

- **Feeling powerful**—aware, proud, respected, appreciated, important, empowered, successful, worthwhile, valuable, confident, good, renewed

- **Feeling peaceful**—nurtured, trusting, loving, tranquil, thoughtful, contented, thankful, secure, serene, lovable, pensive, contemplative, relaxed

- **Feeling joyful**—excited, terrific, energetic, cheerful, hopeful, daring, exhilarated, thrilled, fired up, stimulated, amused, playful, optimistic

- **Feeling scared**—afraid, frightened, confused, rejected, helpless, submissive, insecure, anxious, bewildered, discouraged, insignificant, inadequate, embarrassed, overwhelmed, alone, abandoned, desperate, trapped

- **Feeling mad**—hurt, hostile, angry, selfish, hateful, skeptical, critical, distant, sarcastic, frustrated, jealous, annoyed, irritated, upset, distraught, put-down, unimportant, minimized

- **Feeling sad**—tired, bored, lonely, depressed, out of sorts, ashamed, guilty, sleepy, apathetic, isolated, inferior, stupid, remorseful, hopeless, disillusioned, disappointed, weak, powerless

When a boy can't come up with the words for how a character in a story might feel, or describe how he himself feels about something, ask him to get out the Feeling-Word Thesaurus, find a word that comes close, and start talking from there. Such a tool can be very useful in the counselor's or principal's office.

Kindlon and Thompson (2000) compare the process of becoming emotionally literate to learning to read. First, we master the sounds of the alphabet, then we use that knowledge to understand words and sentences, and eventually to comprehend and appreciate increasingly complex thoughts; ultimately, this enables us to communicate more effectively with others. When it comes to emotions, a boy first understands the emotion of anger. Later, he learns that there are degrees of anger and builds his emotional vocabulary. He can be agitated, upset, furious, frustrated, or filled with rage. Exploring the range and depth of emotions allows the boy to be precise in expressing his emotions and communicating them to others, and to understand and deal with the emotions of others.

Anger: The Default Emotion

The lack of words and the slow processing of emotions sets the stage for boys to be trapped in their own anger, the default emotion for many of them. According to Kindlon and Thompson (2000):

> When school is not a good fit for a boy, when his normal expressions of energy and action routinely meet with negative responses from teachers, he stews in feelings of failure—feelings of sadness, shame and anger, which can be very hard to detect beneath that brash exterior. Unable to "talk out" the emotional pressure, boys typically act out through verbal or physical aggression that walls them off emotionally from others, straining or severing emotional connections to the people and circumstances they find painful. And the worse a boy behaves, the more he invites negative reactions from teachers and other adults. (pp. 43–44)

Conflict is inevitable, but acting out is not. In fact, the consequences for boys' acting out their anger can be quite serious, as they no longer have the luxury their grandfathers had when they engaged in underage drinking or got caught in some other wrongdoing. Forty years ago, boys' misbehavior might have been excused with such statements as "boys will be boys." On other occasions, a parent might have been called, or the police might have given the boys a warning and delivered them home. Today, that same misbehavior is labeled *children committing adult crimes*, and the consequences are often the same as they would be for a thirty-year-old adult (Juszkiewicz, 2000; Myers, 2004; Office of Juvenile Justice and Delinquency Prevention, 2006; Snyder & Sickmund, 2006). Youths tried in adult criminal court:

- Face the same penalties as adults, sometimes including life without parole

- Receive little or no education, mental health treatment, or rehabilitative programming

- Receive an adult criminal record, which may significantly limit their future education and employment opportunities

- Are at greater risk of assault and death in adult jails and prisons with adult inmates

- Are more likely to reoffend than young people not exposed to the negative influences and toxic culture of the adult criminal punishment system (Campaign for Youth Justice, n.d.)

Shame Phobia

Boys' lack of words, coupled with their slow processing of emotions, often sets the stage for them to be negatively influenced and make wrong choices, with little regard for the consequences. They can make these choices in a split second when they're surrounded by other boys and one of them makes a dare (Bámaca & Umaña-Taylor, 2006; Santor, Messervey, & Kusumakar, 2000; Schwartz et al., 1998). This is partly rooted in boys being shame-phobic. Boys will do just about anything to avoid the emotion of shame (Pollack, 1998). To be called a sissy, gay, fag, wimp, wuss, momma's boy, teacher's pet, or geek is the kiss of death for most boys.

Shame is a much deeper emotion than guilt. Guilt results from doing something that you believe is wrong and can usually be rectified by understanding that it was either not your fault or by apologizing. Shame, on the other hand, reflects on who you are rather than something you have done, and it isn't as easily overcome (Levant & Pollack, 2003; Pleck, 1981; Wurmser, 1981). Boys who experience sexual or physical abuse often feel great shame, as if they had done something wrong, but an array of other circumstances or events can trigger this emotion for boys (Slocumb, 2007), including:

- Where one lives
- How one dresses
- Where one's father or mother works
- A parent in prison
- Siblings or parents who are subject to ridicule or taunting
- Poor grammar, inability to speak English, an accent or drawl
- Being retained in school
- Inability to participate financially with the in crowd
- Acne, poor teeth, or poor personal hygiene
- Being over- or underweight
- Lacking athletic ability
- Being shunned by girls
- Confusion over one's sexual identity
- A physical impairment, stuttering, dyslexia, failing courses, being a poor reader
- Being smart, making good grades, being gifted, artistic, or talented in some way

- A name that subjects one to teasing or taunting

- Parents who don't speak English

Many of these issues may be beyond the boy's control, but they can still be sources of shame. No doubt, Devin experienced great shame because of his stuttering, and his father's criticism only intensified that feeling. Being aware of what causes a boy to feel shame can help educators be more sensitive to his needs. If a teacher knows a boy's father is in prison, why ask him what his father does for a living? If a boy is poor, why ask what his family did on summer vacation?

Risk Taking

In Western culture, perceptions of masculinity are often driven by images of strong, macho men (Salisbury & Jackson, 1996). To prove to others that he's just as tough, just as strong as others, a boy becomes a risk taker (Pollack, 1998), and when he feels he cannot measure up to that standard, he experiences shame. For African American, Latino, and Hispanic boys living in poverty, this dynamic can be even stronger, because of the perceived roles that males play in these cultures (Stevenson, 2003). Drug and alcohol abuse, bullying others, belonging to a gang, or even committing a crime become ways for a risk-taking boy who is trying to avoid shame at all costs to prove his maleness (Thornberry, Krohn, Lizotte, Smith, & Tobin, 2003; Weisel, 2002). Although these risks frequently result in disciplinary action in school, they can get a boy status with his peers—or fail to do so. They can have more serious consequences, as well. Boys are experiencing depression at earlier ages, and suicide has become the third leading cause of death among boys in their mid-to-late teens, after accidents and homicides. Males also account for almost nine out every ten alcohol and drug law violations. Kindlon and Thompson (2000) state that boys commit 95 percent of juvenile homicides and are the perpetrators of four out of every five crimes that end up in juvenile court.

Neuropsychologist Deborah Yurgelun-Todd (PBS Parents, n.d.) notes that the frontal lobes of the brain are not always fully functioning in teenagers, leading to poor decision making:

> That would suggest that, therefore, teenagers aren't thinking through what the consequences of their behaviors are, which would lead us to believe that they'd be more impulsive, because they're not going to be so worried about whether or not what they're doing has a negative consequence.

The Legacy of Abuse

Sexual abuse in childhood can disable—even destroy—self-esteem, self-concept, relationships, and the ability to trust. It also can leave a toxic residue of psychological trauma that compromises a boy's confidence in adults. Sexually abused boys face a reduced quality of life, impaired social relationships, less-than-optimal daily functioning, and self-destructive behavior (Valente, 2005) Over the years, physical, sexual, verbal, and emotional abuse have a ripple effect on an individual's emotional interactions and reactions (Mullen, Martin, Anderson, Roman, & Herbison, 1996; Woods & Kingsley, 2003). Research shows that abused and neglected children are 25 percent more likely to experience such problems as delinquency, teen pregnancy, low academic achievement, drug use, and mental health problems (Kelley, Thornberry, & Smith, 1997). Other studies suggest that abused or neglected children are more prone to engage in sexual risk taking as they reach adolescence (Johnson, Rew, & Sternglanz, 2006; Senn, Carey, Vanable, Coury-Doniger, & Urban, 2007).

The following statistics tell the story of child abuse in North America:

- According to estimates in the 1990s in Canada, there were close to 5 million male victims of sexual abuse, most of which consists of unwanted sexual touching (Matthews, 1996).

- In a *Los Angeles Times* poll conducted in 1990 with 2,626 men and women over eighteen years of age, Finkelhor and Associates discovered that 16 percent of the men recalled a history of sexual abuse. The median age for these male victims was 9.9 years of age (as cited in Wiehe, 1998).

- A 2002 study found that one out of six boys in North America is a victim of sexual abuse (Dorais, 2002).

- In a study of thirty male victims of sexual abuse, the average age at the first time of abuse was eight years, four months (Dorais, 2002).

- When researchers surveyed 1,213 students in the sixth to eighth grades in Toronto-area schools on whether they had been a victim of unwanted sexual behaviors in the previous six weeks, 22 percent of the males reported having been victimized (Blackwell, 2002).

- An estimated 905,000 children were victims of child abuse or neglect in 2006 (U.S. Department of Health and Human Services, 2008).

According to a National Institute of Justice study (English, Widom, & Bradford, 2004), abused and neglected children were 11 times more likely to be arrested for criminal behavior as a juvenile, 2.7 times more likely to be arrested for violent and criminal behavior as an adult, and 3.1 times more likely to be arrested for one of many forms of violent crime (juvenile or adult). A Longitudinal Studies of Child Abuse and Neglect (LONGSCAN) study also found a relationship among substantiated child maltreatment, poor academic performance, and classroom functioning for school-aged children (Zolotor et al., 1999).

Child abuse and neglect, in some cases, cause important regions of the brain to fail to form or grow properly, resulting in cognitive delays and impaired development (De Bellis & Thomas, 2003). These alterations in brain maturation have long-term consequences for cognitive, language, and academic abilities (Watts-English, Fortson, Gibler, Hooper, & De Bellis, 2006). As we have seen, these psychological problems can show up as high-risk behaviors, depression, and anxiety, which make a person more likely to smoke, abuse alcohol or illicit drugs, or overeat. These behaviors, in turn, can lead to long-term health problems, such as sexually transmitted diseases, cancer, and obesity (Child Welfare Information Gateway, 2008).

Trauma

Certain feelings become buried in the brain. When they do, clinical depression can follow, usually requiring a combination of medication and psychotherapy (Schriner, 2006). Feelings associated with childhood trauma, however, become stuck in a deeper, more primitive part of the brain (Turner & Stets, 2005). Witnessing a shooting or the devastation of a hurricane, seeing a mother battered, or experiencing sexual abuse may result in such suppressed feelings. When this occurs, events later in life may trigger their recurrence, creating extreme discomfort or depression or producing overt behaviors, a condition labeled *post–traumatic stress syndrome* or *PTSS* (Cohen, Mannarino, & Deblinger, 2006). A psychologist or counselor is usually required to address PTSS by helping the victim label the feeling, attach words to it, and develop coping strategies.

However, children under the age of three or four who experience trauma have insufficient language to recall the feelings associated with the traumatic event recorded in the brain at a sensory level. Most people, in fact, have difficulty recalling even ordinary events and experiences that occurred prior to age four for the same reason—they didn't have enough language at the time (Jones, 1999). Bloom (1996) writes, "Our cognitive processes are dependent on language, and without words we cannot think" (p. 249). If later experiences trigger those feelings, the child will have no cognitive memory of them. When this occurs, the person, with the help of a professional, has to identify those stimulants in the environment that trigger the feeling in order to develop coping strategies.

There is now a growing body of research that suggests that the process of traumatization begins even before birth, making the pregnant mother's experiences critical to the child's emotional development (Osofsky, 1998; Spietz & Kelly, 2002). For example, pregnant mothers who experience stressful and traumatic events experience hormonal changes in the body. The fetus is affected by trauma, just as it is by the mother's use of alcohol.

Regardless of social class, when you have been a victim of physical or emotional abuse, you learn two things, control and manipulation, because they keep you safe. In emotionally healthy families, adults talk to adults; they don't use children. In dysfunctional families, children are often used by the parents, which puts the child in the power seat, a position a child is not ready or able to handle. When information to deliver to another adult is given to a child, the child can intentionally or unintentionally misrepresent the sender, giving the child the power to create conflict. Because it becomes such a habitual resource for dealing with a dysfunctional environment, this strategy is used in almost all relationships. Children who come from divorce are frequently used this way by their parents, especially if the divorce was not amicable and the anger between the two adults has not been resolved ("Well, you can just tell your mother [father] . . ."). Such children learn the skills of manipulation and control but, unfortunately, not the skills of arbitration and conflict resolution. Without them, the child can manipulate or misrepresent people's words. When conflict arises, they may use physical force to resolve the conflict, or try and manipulate the situation by blaming someone else, making excuses, or lying. School personnel also frequently and unwittingly do this as well ("Tell your mother . . . !"). The relationship between teachers and parents can be somewhat analogous to that of divorcing parents. The teacher tells the student to tell his mother how he got that mark on his arm. The child goes home, gives an inaccurate story, and then the parent bounces back with, "Well, you can just tell your teacher if that happens again I am going to . . ." The result: the teacher blames the parent, the parent blames the teacher, and the student is held unaccountable for his actions.

Generational Poverty and Boys' Emotional Development

Generational poverty affects boys' emotional development in the following ways:

- **Unaddressed emotional issues**—Despite the fact that early death is a common occurrence in poverty, grief counseling is seldom available because of a lack of resources or a fear of or inability to work with mental health professionals. There is also a disproportional amount of mental illness in poverty (7 percent as opposed to 3 percent in the middle class). Many people in poverty address these issues through self-medication and use of alcohol, cigarettes, and other substances. Furthermore, if a biochemical addiction or long-repressed abuse issue exists, there is no money to pay for the treatment. Even if the financial resources for counseling and other services could be found, treatment can be difficult for males, in particular, because in generational poverty it is taboo to use the "touchy-feely," "warm and fuzzy language" associated with mental health professionals (Berliner, 2009).

- **Higher incidence of child abuse**—Child abuse is also higher in poverty, seven times the rate reported in middle-class families (Renchler, 1993). According to Lesa Bethea (1999), only 35 percent of reported child abuse cases are actually substantiated, a figure he says could be significantly increased by improved reporting by child protective agencies.

- **Absence of mediation**—As we have noted, boys have less language for expressing their emotions. This is magnified in conditions of poverty, wherein boys tend to exhibit lower language abilities overall (Hart & Risley, 1995). In generational poverty, the process of mediation often doesn't happen. Instead, the adult may hit the child and tell him not to do something. What the child did, why it was inappropriate, and how to show correct behavior in the future are rarely, if ever, discussed. For behavior to change, however, the mediation process must occur. The adult must provide the child with answers to these questions.

- **Negative self-talk**—In poverty, there is less positive language in the environment, and the affirmative self-talk that one needs to complete tasks and deal with difficult situations is in short supply. In many educated households, when a child runs into a difficult task, the parent will sit down, talk about how to do it, and then say, "I know you can. I'll be here to help you." That child embeds the words, "I know you can." We saw that Devin never received such words of encouragement from his father. Instead, he received ridicule. For boys like Devin, the effects of absence of affirmative self-talk show up in school, and in the end, they may just quit.

- **Lack of emotional resources**—Emotional resources are linked to an idea or image of what one's future life could be. Because very few adults or children in poverty have a future story, they typically live in the tyranny of the moment. A future story helps control impulsivity: if I know that I want to be a doctor, then in high school, I'm not going to get drunk or stay out before a major exam that may affect my grades and my ability to get into med school. Emotional resources are also tied to hope, which research shows is a huge asset in developing resiliency. Resiliency is an identifier of highly successful individuals (Goodwin, 2006; Henderson & Milstein, 2003; Sanders, 2000).

- **Lack of dialogue and language for the experience of oneself**—Who the boy is as a person is rarely discussed. The language, time, inclination, or knowledge base just isn't there. There are often neither enough words to name emotions nor the ability to ask syntactically correct questions. Questions are the tools used by the brain to get answers. If you can only make statements, there is no question. Moreover, Annemarie Palinscar and Ann Brown (1984) found that students who could not ask questions syntactically rarely got past the third-grade reading level.

- **Lack of resources for conflict resolution**—Conflict resolution requires that you go from the personal to the issue. To go to the issue, you need vocabulary that allows you to do so. For example, you can fight about who is the best friend or you can argue about what makes a good friend. The first argument becomes very personal. The second is much more issue oriented.

- **Overuse of video games**—Sax (2007, p. 67) writes that "researchers at Yale University recently reported that playing violent video games such as Doom clearly and unambiguously causes young men to have a more violent self image and to behave more violently" (Sax, 2007, p. 67). Furthermore, he goes on to say, "Every investigator who has correlated the amount of time that a child or adolescent or young adult spends playing video games with that student's academic performance has found a negative correlation" (Sax, 2007, p. 63).

Supporting the Emotional Development of Boys

Table 3.1 shows ways to support the emotional development of males that can help them stay engaged in and graduate from high school.

Table 3.1: Supporting Boys' Emotional Development to Prevent Dropout

Preschool Years (birth to age 4)	Teach the vocabulary of emotions.
	Teach appropriate behaviors to be respectful of others.
	Force young children to ask syntactically correct questions. Have them orally practice beginning questions with *who, what, where, how,* and *why.*
Boyhood (ages 5–10, kindergarten –grade 5)	Teach students how to ask questions syntactically (also helps develop better reading skills). The mind doesn't know what it doesn't know if the student cannot formulate questions.
	Teach affirmations and positive self-talk.
	Help students form the basis for a future story with positive statements: "With that beautiful smile, you should consider being a dentist." "You argue very well. You would make a great lawyer."
	Have students complete the Future Story exercise (page 109).
	Provide the phrases and words to resolve conflict.
	Provide counseling.
	Use the Collaboration For Kids program (developed by H. W. Conway, 2006) as a way to provide early interventions using community resources.
	Openly discuss risk taking. When is it beneficial? When is it dangerous?
Adolescence (ages 11–16, grades 6–10)	To better deal with emotions, teach the five steps in the grieving process: denial, anger, bargaining, depression, and acceptance (Kübler-Ross, 1969).
	Teach how one sets up emotional and physical boundaries.
	Embed feeling words in the content, especially science and social studies: "How do you think Christopher Columbus felt when he set sail for the New World? Do you think he was afraid, excited, apprehensive?"
	Provide counseling.
	Have students write a future story: "What skills, attitudes, and behaviors should you practice at school to help you achieve your goals?"
	Provide the phrases and words to resolve conflict.
	To practice formulating syntactically correct questions, have students develop multiple choice questions as part of reviewing for a test.
	Embed question making into academic tasks.
	Provide academic coaching and relational learning.
	Develop a classroom Feeling-Word Thesaurus.
	Openly discuss risk taking. When is it beneficial? When is it dangerous?
Early Manhood (ages 17–23, grade 11 to post–high school)	Provide discussions about dealing with death, disappointment, the loss of a relationship, and so on.
	Discuss boundaries at work and in personal relationships.
	Provide tools for anger management.
	Model the adult voice rather than a critical, judgmental voice. Ask questions and clarify responses ("What I hear you saying is . . .").
	Identify patterns of verbal disrespect and ways to know when another person has moved from criticism to contempt.

4 The Cognitive Development of Boys

This chapter looks at the basic organization of the brain, at cognitive differences between boys and girls, and at the windows of opportunity that open in the brain at various stages of development. We also explore the effects of generational poverty on cognitive development and suggest interventions that will support boys' cognitive development and help them to remain in and succeed at school.

Brain Physiology and Cognition

Research in the area of Alzheimer's disease, strokes, brain injuries, and learning disabilities since the 1980s has produced a body of knowledge about the human brain that didn't exist twenty-five years ago. We now know that the brain has about a trillion cells and that they fall into one of two categories: (1) nerve cells, or neurons, which represent one-tenth of the total number of cells, roughly 100 billion, and (2) glial (from the Greek word for *glue*), which holds neurons together and filters out substances harmful to them.

Neuron development in the brain begins in the embryo during the first four months of gestation. However, about half of the neurons that develop fail to connect and die off by the fifth month of gestation. This prevents the brain from becoming overcrowded with unconnected cells (Sousa, 2000). Drugs or alcohol that the mother might consume during pregnancy increase the risk of neurological defects as well as addiction in the unborn child (American Council for Drug Education, n.d.).

Branches that develop on the neurons, known as *dendrites*, receive electrical impulses through a long fiber known as the *axon*. There is usually one axon per neuron, which is protected by a layer called the *myelin sheath*. The axon controls the speed at which the impulses are transmitted. Between the dendrite and axon is a small gap called the *synapse* (a Greek word meaning "to join together"). Impulses travel along the axon, across the synapses, to the dendrites of a nearby cell. Brain development is impacted by the features of the environment, including such factors as language acquisition, diet, toxins, and so on.

The prefrontal cortex of the brain, located just behind the forehead, acts as the brain's executive control center. Cox (2007) compares the prefrontal cortex to a symphony orchestra, regulating higher-order thinking and problem solving and interfacing with the emotional system. According to Cox, executive control is involved in such tasks as "getting started on something, sustaining attention, remembering critical information, and monitoring one's own actions" (p. 4). Working memory is located in the frontal lobes of the brain. This area develops slowly over a period of years (Durston et al., 2001).

As the child approaches puberty, the brain's learning pace slows down, and two other processes begin: connections the brain finds useful become permanent, whereas connections the brain doesn't find useful are eliminated.

Windows of Opportunity

Although it continues throughout life, the process of strengthening or pruning neural connections based on usefulness is most intense between the ages of three and twelve. During this peak development time, there are windows of opportunity during which the brain responds to certain types of input to create neural networks. If the brain doesn't receive certain stimuli at the appropriate times, these networks don't develop (Sousa, 2006). For example, if an infant doesn't receive visual stimuli prior to age two, that child will be blind. If the child does not hear words, he or she will rarely develop oral language.

Once the windows of opportunity taper off, the brain's ability to perform certain tasks diminishes. Learning can occur throughout life, but the skill level will probably not be as high. Table 4.1 gives a graphic representation of Sousa's windows of opportunity.

Delayed Language Acquisition

A huge difference between boys' and girls' cognitive development is boys' delay in language acquisition (Baron-Cohen et al., 2004; Feingold, 1993; Halpern, 2000; Hyde & Linn, 1988). In "Gender Differences in Cognitive Functioning," Heidi Weiman (2004) writes:

> Behaviorally, females have consistently shown an advantage for verbal abilities, including earlier language acquisition and longer attention spans

than males for conversation (as cited in Kruger, 2001). Females also tend to excel at memory tasks, including associational fluency, which includes generating synonyms, as well as color naming, or listing items beginning with a designated letter (Halpern, 2000; Kimura, 1992). The underlying cognitive process appears to involve rapid retrieval of information from memory. Females also tend to excel at tasks involving manual dexterity and perceptual speed, such as visually identifying matching items.

Most girls develop their verbal skills as much as one to two years ahead of boys (Neu & Weinfeld, 2007). Simon Baron-Cohen (2003) reports that girls' speech is more interactive and reciprocal and that girls verbalize their feelings more quickly. This male developmental lag is often ignored in schools: whether a boy is five years and eleven months old or has just rounded the corner to five when he starts school, the expectations of the curriculum are the same. The developmental lag sets the stage for trouble in the areas of reading and writing in boys' early years. A boy who struggles in those first years of school, even though he may catch up by third grade, tends to form negative attitudes about school that never go away. In order to protect their sons from this early experience of failure, many middle-class parents deliberately hold them back from entering kindergarten for a year.

Table 4.1: Windows of Opportunity for Neural Networks

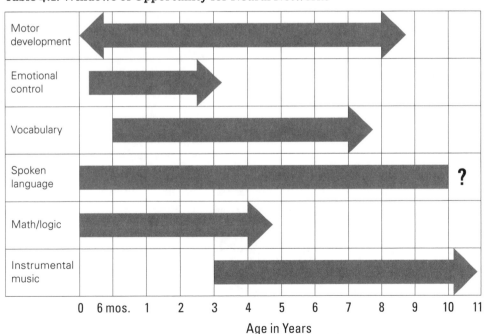

Adapted from *How the Brain Learns*, by David Sousa, Corwin, 2000, p.25. Used with permission.

The Crucial Importance of Vocabulary Instruction

Boys' delay in language acquisition can be countered with vocabulary instruction. In fact, the strongest action a teacher can take to ensure that all students understand the content they will encounter in school is to provide direct instruction in vocabulary. Without an understanding of the words, it is difficult for students to grasp the information they will read and hear (Marzano & Pickering, 2005). According to Robert Marzano's (2004) five-step process to teach vocabulary, teachers should perform the following steps:

1 Present a brief explanation of the new term or phrase.

2 Present a nonlinguistic representation of the new term or phrase.

3 Ask the students to generate their own explanations or descriptions of the new term or phrase.

4 Ask the students to create their own nonlinguistic representation of the term or phrase.

5 Periodically ask students to review the accuracy of their explanation or terms.

Along with self-image and self-esteem, a child's vocabulary, more than any single factor, will determine how successful he or she will be in school and in life. According to John Pikulski and Shane Templeton (2004):

> It seems almost impossible to overstate the power of words; they literally have changed and will continue to change the course of world history. Perhaps the greatest tools we can give students for succeeding, not only in their education but more generally in life, is a large, rich vocabulary and the skills for using those words. (p. 1)

Abstract Learning

With growing accountability for schools and the increased challenges of a more global and competitive workplace, schools have demanded more from students at ever earlier ages (Goldstein, 2007; Hatch, 2004). However, because many boys tend to lag behind girls developmentally in the areas of reading, writing, and verbal ability, for them, some learning simply comes too soon.

Schools now require students in kindergarten to begin acquiring formal reading and writing skills by midyear. Again, boys born two or three months prior to the official start date age are at a disadvantage. To come from poverty is an even greater disadvantage. Even though they lag behind, boys from impoverished environments are expected to meet the requirements. In Finland, which has the highest literacy rate in the world and a very low poverty rate, students begin school at seven years of age (Sax, 2007).

Other Cognitive Differences

Language differences between boys and girls are relatively easy to spot, but other cognitive differences are more subtle. For example, boys tend to be deductive thinkers; girls are more likely to think inductively (Gurian & Henley, 2001). Boys would prefer to be given the generalization or theory, and then look for the examples. Because boys' cognitive strength is in their spatial ability, they tend to be better in mathematical problem solving and reasoning than girls, who are better at computation (Geary, 1996). Boys prefer hands-on learning versus oral and written lessons (Gurian & Henley, 2001; Neu & Weinfeld, 2007).

Boys are also single-task focused, whereas girls tend to be better at multitasking (Spence, Booth, & Walters, 2008). Some researchers believe that this difference is connected to the size of the corpus callosum, which is larger in girls compared to boys (Moir & Jessel, 1992). A larger corpus callosum enables greater cross-talk between the left and right hemispheres of the brain, allowing girls to switch hemisphere functions with ease. The size of the passageway explains why boys don't want to let a task go once they have taken it on, a characteristic of boys' cognition that is sometimes interpreted as stubbornness or an unwillingness to follow directions.

Relationships and Cognition

A child's cognitive capacity—the ability to pay attention, learn, and use and interpret information—begins in the context of relationships. In fact, nurturing relationships can change genetic activity! Canadian scientist Michael Meaney has shown that how much a mother rat licks and grooms her newborns during the first twelve hours after birth determines how brain chemicals will respond for the rest of the rat's life. Goleman (2006) writes:

> The more nurturing the mother, the more quick-witted, confident and fearless the pup will become; the less nurturing she is, the slower to learn and more overwhelmed by threats the pup will be. . . . The pups born to devoted mothers, who licked and groomed the most, grew up to have denser connections between their brain cells, particularly in the hippocampus, the seat of memory and learning. (p. 253)

This isn't just true of rats, says Daniel Goleman: "The human equivalents of licking and grooming seem to be empathy, attunement, and touch" (p. 253). Parental nurture, specifically touching and stroking, is essential for normal neuronal growth. Stroking stimulates the production of chemicals that inhibit the stress hormones, including cortisol, that kill neurons (Howard, 2006). Poverty is a stressful environment. When there is constant crisis, there is less time for nurturing.

Double Coding

All learning is double coded. That is, content enters the brain simultaneously through two channels, a cognitive channel and an emotional channel. Learning is therefore directly related to relationships (Greenspan & Benderly, 1997). Likewise, how we respond is also double coded—responses have both cognitive and emotional content.

Once boys are in school, building cognitive capacity requires a combination of curriculum and instruction (content) and motivation through relationships (emotion). Educators must build these early. Developmental studies show that by the third grade, most children have established the patterns of learning that will shape their entire school career (Alexander & Entwisle, 1988). In Goleman's book *Social Intelligence* (2006), he cites a study done with 910 first graders. If the at-risk students in these classrooms perceived the teacher to be cold and controlling, they refused to learn from the teacher.

Physical Activity and Learning

Unfortunately, a number of trends are changing schools in ways that works against boys' developmental needs. Two of the most important are the downward push of skills to younger and younger students, along with the cutting back and in some cases virtual elimination of physical activity.

The increased focus on early literacy has decreased the amount of time devoted to physical education, recess, or unstructured play during the school day (Rhea, 2009). In 1987, researchers warned that physical education in schools in the United States was an endangered species (Siedentop, 1987). Now, over twenty years later, only about 25 percent of students attend physical education class daily or take part in any daily physical activity—but boys have not stopped needing physical activity. Moreover, the percentage of children who are overweight or obese more than doubled between 1970 and 2000 (National Association for Sport and Physical Education, 2000).

Intensive physical activity actually enhances and increases learning. John J. Ratey, a researcher from Harvard, argues that during cognitively, socially, and aerobically demanding physical activity, the brain produces what he calls "miracle grow" chemicals and structures that help one learn even more (Ratey & Hagerman, 2007; Sattelmair & Ratey, 2009). Jacob Sattelmair and John Ratey describe studies with compelling findings, such as the following:

- Body mass index and physical activity, together, explain up to 24 percent of variance in academic achievement (Sigfusdottir, Kristjansson, & Allegrante, 2007, cited in Sattelmair & Ratey, 2009).

- Academic ratings were significantly correlated with exercise levels and performance on physical fitness tests (Dwyer, Coonan, Leitch, Hetzel, & Baghurst, 1983, cited in Sattelmair & Ratey, 2009).

- When school officials in Titusville, Pennsylvania, set up an appropriate physical education program, standardized test scores went "from below the state average to 17 and 18 percent above average in reading and math, respectively. The incidents of fighting . . . dropped dramatically" (Sattelmair & Ratey, 2009, p. 371).

- After one year of daily physical education, students at Woodland Elementary School in Kansas City, Missouri, showed dramatically improved fitness measures, as well as a 67 percent drop in suspensions from the previous year, reduced academic probation, and improved literacy (PE4life, 2007).

Head Trauma

Because the brain is still developing during childhood and adolescence, and because boys tend to be greater risk takers, they are more vulnerable to injuries that can result in cognitive impairment. Margie Patlak and Janet Joy (2002) write that "youths who experience concussions may be more at risk for brain damage than adults, because their brains are still developing and have unique features that heighten their susceptibility to serious consequence from head injuries" (p. 1). They point out that even sports considered relatively safe, like soccer, present dangers when the head is not protected:

Even though people generally think that soccer is a safer sport than football, soccer players experience concussions about as often as football players. Concussions are usually caused by head collisions with players, goalposts, or the ground. Soccer players frequently use their unprotected heads to pass or shoot the ball. A soccer ball can hit the head with significant force, and there has been considerable debate over whether such "heading" also fosters brain injury. (Patlak & Joy, 2002, p. 1)

The risk of head trauma is increased in children who don't wear helmets while riding bicycles and motorcycles. Thus, during adolescence, when adolescent boys tend to engage in risky behavior, there is an increased likelihood of head injuries and cognitive impairment.

Generational Poverty and Boys' Cognitive Development

Generational poverty exacerbates problems with the development of cognition in boys in the following ways:

- **Low birth weight**—A disproportionate number of babies in poverty are born with low birth weight, which has an impact on brain development (Berliner, 2009).

- **Allostatic load**—This is a measure of the body's responses to stressors in the environment (instability, food insecurity, violence, addiction, lack of safety, and so on). The greater the body's reaction to the stressors, the greater the interference with working memory—the ability to remember one thing while you work on something else.

- **Substance abuse**—Alcohol, tobacco, and cocaine use are higher in poor neighborhoods (Berliner, 2009).

- **Exposure to environmental toxins (air, lead, mercury)**—Toxins include mercury in food, lead, PCBs (chemical dioxins), pesticides, and air quality. Less-expensive neighborhoods often have more of these toxins in the immediate environment. These toxins impact physical well-being and learning (Berliner, 2009).

- **Food insecurity and hunger**—Food is the fuel of the brain; and when it isn't available, the brain doesn't function very well. Twelve million American children experience food insecurity (Feeding America, 2009). The amount of protein that one receives is directly related to the development of the myelin sheath in the brain, a factor in basic intelligence (Sousa, 2003). Gurian (1999) reports that because food intake has an impact on brain processing, "chronic conditions during male life, from depression to addiction to mental illness to violence, are being at least partially treated through the monitoring of food intake" (p. 82).

- **Language deprivation**—An Australian study (Najman et al., 2004) that followed the children of 8,556 women, mostly from poverty, found that the occupational status of the child's maternal grandfathers independently predicted the child's verbal comprehension levels at the age of five and the verbal reasoning scores at the age of fourteen. A study by Betty Hart and Todd Risley (1995) found that children in poverty hear 13 million words from their parents by the time they are four years old, while in professional households, children hear 45 million words during the same time period. These researchers found that most four-year-olds in professional households have more vocabulary than adults in welfare households.

Another factor is that, because few low-income families can afford the costs of childcare to keep a son at home for an additional year to compensate for boys' normal developmental lag in language acquisition, many boys, especially those from poverty, end up being placed in special programs. Eighth-grade boys are twice as likely as girls to be held back a grade, and two thirds of high school special education students are boys (Gurian, 2006).

- **Absence of emotional connection and touch**—Because most learning occurs within the context of relationships, if the primary caretaker, educated or not, is preoccupied with survival and is emotionally unresponsive to the child during the first two years of life, cognitive development is delayed. How do you develop emotional responses when there isn't a vocabulary for them and there are only physical responses, or when the caregiver is working two jobs to survive? Further, we know that cognitive development is greatly enhanced in young children by being held. A great deal of research indicates that children who are not touched very much develop serious delays cognitively and emotionally.

- **Fear and scarcity**—The world of poverty is largely based on fear and scarcity: "If I go to the grocery store with two dollars, I can buy this or this—but not both." Over time, the mind reduced to these kinds of choices doesn't see options anymore, only polarities: everything becomes either/or, not both/and. When there's very little money in the house and virtually no discussion of how to count it, which is often a middle-class child's introduction to math, how can a child understand math and logic? Fear and scarcity also produce negative self-talk— "I can't have that," or, "I can't do that." Hart & Risley (1995) found that in generational poverty, parents make two negative comments for every positive one, whereas in professional households parents make six positive comments for every negative one.

- **Undeveloped executive function**—The environment of extreme poverty requires a child to be reactive and nonverbal and to pay close attention to sensory data; the environment of school requires the student to be proactive, live in a world of abstract representations (paper, computers), and use language to express thinking and feeling. For boys in poverty, these two worlds are diametrically opposed. The University of California at Berkeley did research using MRI (magnetic resonance imaging) scans to compare the brains of nine- and ten-year-old poor children with middle-class children of the same ages (Kishiyama, Boyce, Jimenez, Perry, & Knight, 2009). Mark Kishiyama, the lead researcher, indicated that the patterns in poor children's brains were similar to those of adults who have had strokes and, therefore, have lesions in their prefrontal cortex. The prefrontal cortex controls executive functions: working memory, behavioral self-regulation, cognitive control, reward processing, and problem-solving ability. It follows, then, that if a parent came from poverty, the executive functions likely would not be as well developed and so could not be passed on to the children. You can't teach what you don't know.

- **Under- and overstimulation**—If you're in a thousand-square-foot apartment with five other people, and it's too dangerous to be outside, you do not develop as many motor skills, because space is limited. Books are less available. Musical instruments, games, puzzles, and other tools and supports may not be available. The quality of your surroundings, even the light and contrasting color in the living space, are directly correlated to visual discrimination (Gurian & Stevens, 2005).

- **Living in an abstract representational world**—School and work are about the ability to live in a world where ideas are represented through drawings and words, and these ideas are often decontextualized; in other words, the natural environment for learning is in context with tasks, language, relationships, and socially negotiated meaning. But in formal schooling, learning is decontextualized, and ideas are represented on paper through letters and numbers and drawings. Therefore, music and art are wonderful tools to teach some of these ideas.

Supporting the Cognitive Development of Boys

Table 4.2 shows some strategies for developing cognitive capacity for males in order to help them stay engaged in and graduate from high school.

Table 4.2: Supporting Boys' Cognitive Development to Prevent Dropout

Preschool Years (birth to age 4)	Use a kinesthetic approach to teaching whenever possible. Hands-on learning—things that can be manipulated—works better with most boys. Provide kinesthetic tools to teach the alphabet (symbols) and sounds (for example, Tucker Signing Strategies, which combines signing letters with letter sounds and blending those sounds to decode words).
	Use drawings to teach how things are alike and different, a prerequisite skill for comparing and contrasting (which are highly correlated to achievement) as well as for categorizing, summarizing, and sorting information.
	Use sketching to teach vocabulary. The brain has a limited ability to remember words but almost an unlimited ability to remember pictures.
Boyhood (ages 5–10, kindergarten –grade 5)	*Never* eliminate recess, music, or art. Music and art teach how sounds, time, and counting are represented abstractly on paper. Boys need movement, and recess provides an opportunity for students to move around (Ratey & Hagerman, 2007).
	Teach dance. Dance teaches counting, patterns of melody, and time—and provides movement.
	Use mental models to teach concepts and ideas. Mental models are stories, analogies, or drawings that translate abstract ideas to sensory realities and speed up learning.
	Teach question making—a prerequisite skill for accessing memory.
	Have active students sit on Pilates balls instead of chairs. (Sitting on the balls requires constant subtle movement to stay balanced and helps some students learn more.)
	Use movement techniques for learning.
	Teach simple planning techniques.
	Teach formal register and sentence structure. Explicit, precise language is essential to negotiate and manipulate one's position in the world. Implicit language is vague and leaves a person vulnerable to interpretation. "This sucks" is vivid, but it does not communicate as much as "Ms. Johnson, I don't understand what we're supposed to do."
Adolescence (ages 11–16, grades 6–10)	Build in daily physical activity (for example, line and square dancing at lunch).
	Have students work in groups. All learning is double coded cognitively and emotionally. Emotions are stimulated through relationships.
	Use mental models and relational learning.
	Educate parents on the harmful effects of video games on behavior and achievement.
	Make key lessons available on video and MP3 downloads.
	Have students develop multiple-choice test questions (two of the highest levels of Bloom's taxonomy) to improve critical thinking.
	Teach processes for nonfiction text and math problem solving.
	Teach backwards planning. Start with the goal, the finished product, and then define the steps that will help students reach that goal.

continued on next page →

Early Manhood (ages 17–23, grade 11 to post–high school)	Use all of the techniques listed here, as well as time and task management. (Issues related to early manhood are addressed in chapter 8, "Emerging Adulthood," page 85). Teach backward planning, as described above, putting the emphasis on reaching a goal. Work with high school seniors who are going to attend a community college to encourage them to buddy with another student attending the same college.

5 The Social Development of Boys

In this chapter, we look at patterns of socialization in boys' social development, including the roles of aggression and competition and the influence of media as a provider—sometimes the only provider—of role models for boys. We examine ways that generational poverty affects boys' socialization patterns and suggest supports for boys' social development to help them remain in school.

Patterns of Socialization

Boys and girls aren't born knowing what it means to be men and women. They must be taught through interactions with others. They learn this in a variety of ways: through observation and imitation, coercion and persuasion, reward and punishment, instruction and example (Chevannes, 2001). Adolescence is typically the staging ground for this initiation and integration into the larger adult society, with its roles and responsibilities. Anthropologists have studied the process of coming of age in cultures around the globe, and almost everywhere, they have found that socialization has traditionally been the responsibility of single-gendered communities. Girls learned from the women in the community, and boys learned from men—and not just their mothers and fathers. The process of passing on a culture, with its rules, norms, beliefs, and expectations, traditionally involves the larger community (Sax, 2007; Tiger, 2004).

In earlier generations, fathers went fishing or hunting with their sons, and boys focused on learning a trade from other men through the apprentice system (Rorabaugh, 1988). In modern times, this community is approximated by pairing boys with responsible adult males, for example, in woodworking classes (Marusza, 2004). Many boys have also participated in single-gender organizations, such as the Boy Scouts or boys club, or attended all-male camps, where they were exposed to adult models of masculinity (Mechling, 2001; Hantover, 1978).

Family structure has changed, however. Over the last thirty to forty years, many activities that were single-gendered have all but disappeared in our culture. Today, parents shoulder much of the socialization process, and many single moms struggle just to provide the essentials for their children. Single parenthood is especially problematic for children's socialization, because the single adult's time is so limited. Children with one parent often receive less economic and emotional support, practical assistance, information, guidance, supervision, and role modeling than children in two-parent families (Amato, 1993). Grandparents may live thousands of miles away from their grandchildren. Many fathers are completely absent from their children's lives. A study of children from families disrupted by divorce across three generations concluded that these children "lose something fundamental to their development—family structure, the scaffolding upon which children mount successive developmental stages, which supports their psychological, physical and emotional ascent into maturity" (Abbott, Meredith, Self-Kelly, & Davis, 1997, p. 144).

Role and Gender Identity

Both role identity and gender identity are developed as part of the socialization process. *Role identity* is about what you do, the part you play in the larger society—"I am a teacher," "I am a fireman," "I am a policeman." In families, the roles are mother, father, son, daughter, grandmother, uncle, and so on. In contemporary society, and particularly in poverty, boys and girls are often without immediate role models.

Gender identity is what you think a man or woman is—what it means to be masculine or feminine. Regardless of his or her sexual orientation, a child's gender identity is critical to healthy development.

Sax (2007) explains the problem of identity in boys this way:

> If a boy does not have a community of men, then he is likely to look else-where for his role models. In seeking a "tribe" to which he can belong, many boys end up involved with drugs, alcohol, or gangs—or in trouble with the law. Or he may look to the media, where he will encounter a bliz-zard of images of men like Eminem and Akon and 50 Cent—all of whom make their money by writing songs that are degrading to women. He may look to his peers, to boys his own age. The results of teenage boys

looking to other teenage boys for guidance are often confused and self-destructive. Teenage boys are seldom competent to guide one another to manhood. (p. 170)

Boys need relationships with adults who offer support, have high expectations, insist on quality work, and enforce social and emotional behaviors. Boys need relationships with teachers that are based on mutual respect. Students believe they are respected when adults challenge them to succeed academically, give attention to their particularities and commonalities, are responsive to their needs, and foster positive expectations (Hajii, 2006; Jones, 2002; Pierce, 1994). Hajii (2006) writes further that respect is essential for success in school; it helps students experience positive feedback, empowerment, and self-worth.

Aggression and competitiveness are observable traits of most young boys at a very early age, and as they approach adolescence, these characteristics intensify (Coie & Dodge, 1998; Hyde, 2005). However, with the absence of fathers and other appropriate male role models, many boys, particularly those from poverty, are left floundering, unable to channel their aggression and competitiveness in positive ways. Their aggressive and competitive behaviors then become problematic, especially in the school setting, where these behaviors tend to receive a great deal of attention. A boy who has difficulty complying with classroom rules often spends far more time in the principal's or counselor's office, often missing valuable instruction time, than one who complies. Over time, the noncompliant student falls behind others academically and exhibits aggressive and competitive behaviors more frequently.

There is another reason adolescent boys fail: few electives exist for the fourteen-year-old ninth-grade student, and the instruction provided often doesn't take into account his developmental needs. Once a boy has experienced failure, it becomes increasingly difficult for him to catch up to his peers, lengthening the odds that he will drop out. With added emphasis on academic rigor and state competency testing, along with the elimination of hands-on vocational courses, many boys today draw the conclusion that school is a "girl thing," not a "guy thing."

Maturity Levels

The maturity level of most seventeen- and eighteen-year-old boys is significantly different than the maturity level displayed by seventeen- or eighteen-year-old girls (Young Adult Development Project, 2005). Many boys feel the pressure to grow up and be a man, yet have no idea what they want to do with their lives. While striving to be independent, they often don't know how to move from dependence on family to dependence on self, especially if college isn't their chosen path. Boys who grow up in foster care must go out into the world at eighteen, ready or not, with very little additional support from social services (Courtney, 2005).

While many boys are floundering with no sense of direction, girls are pursuing college degrees and careers at a greater rate. According to Britz (2006), "Two-thirds of colleges and universities report that they get more female than male applicants, and more than 56 percent of undergraduates nationwide are women."

Teacher-Student Relationships

Boys aren't as likely as girls to do homework, participate in class, or generally do what the teacher wants just to please. Girls tend to try harder than boys, and do want to please the teacher (Duckworth & Seligman, 2006; Mau & Lynn, 2000; Rogers & Hallam, 2006; Valeski & Stipek, 2001; Xu, 2006). Girls are also more likely than boys to accept the teacher's perspective on their schoolwork. In general, girls are much more likely to affiliate with adults. Anthropologists and other researchers believe this is due to the fact that, in most (but not all) societies, females tend to remain with the family, while males leave (Lindahl & Heimann, 1997; Pereira & Fairbanks, 2002).

Boys' propensity to challenge the teacher is also consistent with recent research that shows that the reaction to stress most of us learned about in school—flight or fight—applies mostly to boys. Girls have a tendency to turn to each other in stressful situations, a trait that researcher Shelley Taylor has called "tend and befriend" (Taylor, 2006).

Boys' first allegiance is usually to other boys. In the classroom, if something is wrong, boys are less likely to tell an adult, whether it's a personal concern or a potentially dangerous event. James McGee and Caren DeBernardo (1999) found that in twenty cases when students intervened to stop a planned school shooting, eighteen of the interveners were girls.

Influence of Media on Socialization

Media are increasingly playing a central role in all children's socialization. In addition to print media, television, recorded music, video, and DVDs, children now have access to electronic games, computer software, and the Internet, along with an interactive element that was not present before. According to the American Academy of Pediatrics (2001), children are influenced by media because they learn by observing, imitating, and making behaviors their own. During the 1980s and 1990s, the unprecedented growth that occurred in the field of computer technology contributed to the expanded media influence on children, especially in less-educated households. In 2001, 73 percent of children whose mothers were college graduates were read to every day, compared to only 42 percent of children whose mothers had not finished high school (Benson, 2003).

Media Messages

During the final two decades of the twentieth century, media content also underwent a transformation characterized by increased use of sexual themes and violent behavior. Research has confirmed the negative effects of media content on children with regard to violence, aggressive behavior, sexuality, body image, self-esteem, physical health, and school performance (Bushman & Huesmann, 2001; Freeman, 2002; Polce-Lynch, Myers, Kliewer, & Kilmartin, 2001).

Though many parents have stressed to their daughters that they can be anything they wish in life, commercial TV messages still sell females on the importance of physical appearance—from hair to perfume to clothing. Girls must look sexy. The emphasis is on the external. Boys, on the other hand, must be impossibly powerful supermen. If a male is portrayed in the media as a family man, he will most likely be the amusing, bumbling idiot in a family sitcom. The message to boys is that they must have a woman to tell them when to come in out of the rain and that they are stupid. In an odd reversal from just a few decades ago, it is women, not men, who are presented as logical and rational.

For girls, the messages are equally as stereotypical and misleading. It's okay to be sarcastic with your husband, to call him names, to put him down in front of his children; in short, it's okay to bully your spouse. Even on *The Cosby Show*, it is the mother, an attorney, who is the more logical and rational one, despite the fact that Dad is a physician. The sitcom *George Lopez* illustrates a similar pattern.

Because it's often the media that teach boys in poverty what it means to be a man, it's vital to look closely at the messages being communicated. Here are several more (Slocumb, 2007):

- If you have an enemy, it will most likely be another male. (Competitiveness is hard-wired in the brains of most boys.)

- Destroy your enemy. (You must win!)

- It's a cruel world, with people who are out to cheat and destroy you and those you love. (When there are few words to articulate one's feelings, emotions rule).

- If you cry, you better do it alone. (Be brave, and never let anyone see your weakness.)

- Females are sexual objects who are meant to be seduced. (Sex is the concrete, sensory-based definition of manhood.)

- The male must be physically fit. Females are attracted to the good-looking jock. (The male must strut and show his colors.)

These messages are significant because, as we have seen, the adolescent male brain processes everything, but is often incapable of evaluating what it takes in. You can't read without thinking, but you can watch TV all day long and *never* think . . . unless there is someone, usually an adult, who can ask probing questions, like the following:

- "Do you really think those shoes will make you run faster?"

- "Why do you think someone would spend over 2 million dollars for a 45-second commercial during the Super Bowl?"

- "Do you ever hear me talking to your mom [dad] that way?"

- "Have you ever noticed how quickly they read the side effects of a drug in those pharmaceutical commercials?"

While adults may be able to distinguish fact from fiction, children aren't always so savvy. As Renee Hobbs contends:

> Just because our students can use media and technology doesn't mean they are effective at critically analyzing and evaluating the messages they receive. Students need a set of skills to ask important questions about what they watch, see, listen to and read. Often called media literacy, these skills include the ability to critically analyze media messages and the ability to use different kinds of communication technologies for self-expression and communication. (2000)

Parental Oversight

The extent to which children are influenced by the media is directly related to the extent of parental supervision over media exposure. Increasingly, boys are secluding themselves in their rooms to watch television alone and to play video games for hours at a time. Three out of five video gamers are males. Sixty-five percent of U.S. households play video games. The average time spent per week by gamers playing video games is eighteen hours (Online Education, 2009). Moreover, poverty is no barrier to television. Television, in fact, is highly valued in poverty. We once polled a middle-school group of students in Cincinnati (where the poverty rate is roughly 85 percent), asking how many of them had a TV in their bedrooms. Eighty percent of the audience raised their hands. Even when boys don't have their own rooms, there is a television in the house, often a big-screen TV.

In 1994, the U.S. Department of Education published guidelines advising parental oversight in this area:

> Parental monitoring is a key factor, since the research studies show that increasing guidance from parents is at least as important as simply reducing media violence. Children may learn negative behavior patterns and values from many other experiences as well as TV programs, and parental guidance is needed to help children sort out these influences and develop the ability to make sound decisions on their own. (p. 1)

Desensitization

Archibald Hart (2007), in his book *Thrilled to Death*, warns that this generation is "thrilled to death," and that the stimulation received from the PDA, Game Boy, PSP, BlackBerry, iPod, and portable DVD and MP3 players is exhilarating and addictive. "Our desire for excitement has become an addiction," he argues, "and as in all addictions, our brain adapts to the present level of stimulation, gets bored with it, and then looks for more . . . more . . . and more!" (p. 167). The result, especially for boys, is that not much shocks them anymore. The brain has, in effect, been desensitized to the horrors of the world. A school counselor shared with us that her son walked through their living room just as the news was showing people jumping from the World Trade Center on 9/11. "Oh, cool," he said. Stunned, the woman realized that her son belonged to a generation that had seen far more blood, guts, and gore on TV than were shown in real life on that one day. Why would he be shocked?

According to Gurian (1998) in *A Fine Young Man*:

> One of the prevailing contemporary theories as to why we in America suffer such high rates of depression, thought disorders (for example, schizophrenia), and brain disorders (for example, ADHD) is that our media technology environment is too stimulating for our brains, whose process of neurotransmitters still runs at a "sane" pace, one that is more appropriate to the stimulation of a few hundred years ago. Media imagery runs at an "insane" pace—that is to say, the stimulation of today is too much for the brain. (p. 220)

Hart (2007) purports that the sensationalism promoted and fed by the media not only elevates the stress hormones of adrenaline and cortisol, but also leads to high cholesterol, heart disease, depression, and anxiety (especially anxiety disorder). Moreover, he writes:

> Sensation seeking is also related to a variety of sexual perversions, the use of illegal drugs (experimentation with drugs in the quest for the higher fix), unhealthy food preferences (that can cause obesity, and other health problems), and risky behaviors (such as dangerous or extreme sports that provide an adrenaline rush). (pp. 168–169)

Entertainment is important in the culture of poverty. It becomes a way of coping—"Life is tough; you've got to have a little fun." Boys in poverty typically lack the parental supervision to censor television viewing and control the use of video games, increasing the aggression of these boys who are already prone to acting impulsively.

Boys Who Don't Fit the Norms

Roy Baumeister and Mark Leary (1995) have argued that the need to belong represents a "fundamental human motivation" (p. 497). Adolescents who feel valued and comfortable in their peer groups have fewer personal and academic problems. A recent study found that boys' sense of belonging in school significantly predicted academic outcomes, including academic motivation, effort, and absenteeism (Sánchez, Colon, & Esparza, 2005). Given evidence that half of all lifetime cases of mental illness begin by the age of fourteen (Egan & Asher, 2005), researchers have argued that the role of a sense of group belonging must be given greater attention as it relates to adolescent adjustment (Brown, 2004; Buhrmester, 1990; Cauce, 1986; Dishion & Owen, 2002; Hirsch & DuBois, 1992; Kiesner, Cadinu, Poulin, & Bucci, 2002; Newman, Lohman & Newman, 2007).

Because of boys' developmental need for more space to process their emotions, they tend to form larger groups than girls (Benenson & Heath, 2006; Geary, Byrd-Craven, Hoard, Vigil, & Numtee, 2003; Tannen, 1991; Turner, 1977). Gurian (2006) suggests that

> large groups create a larger circle of energy and influence through which the boy can exercise his need for more space and physical activity. Large groups are also a better place for a being with a brain that does not process hard emotive data too quickly—the large group allows that brain to shut off and turn on as needed, whereas a dyadic relationship requires the emotional faculties of that brain to be on constantly. (pp. 37–38)

Given the preference for large groups, boys who aren't into sports may experience a more difficult time, as the alternatives aren't that plentiful. Gifted boys, the geeks and nerds, and sensitive and gay boys experience even greater socialization pressures. Being different, in a world where jocks rule, places them in a vulnerable position, especially during adolescence. They're often shunned, ridiculed, or taunted by other boys. Girls who befriend these boys in elementary school often abandon them in middle school, when the girls realize that most of the more popular boys don't like boys who are different. Some of the gifted boys begin to "dumb themselves down" so they'll fit in with the larger male group (Gurian & Stevens, 2005; Pollack, 1998). They refuse to perform academically because it isn't cool to be smart. These themes are explored in greater depth in chapter 7, "The Different Boy: Sensitive, Gay, Gifted, ADHD" (page 73).

Generational Poverty and Boys' Social Development

Generational poverty negatively affects boys' social development in the following ways:

- **Lack of bridging and bonding capital**—Robert Putnam (2000) in *Bowling Alone*, defines the concepts of social bridging capital and bonding capital. People you know who are different from you constitute your bridging capital. Bonding capital is made up of people you know who are like you. To be a poor male means that the majority of adults you see or know in your neighborhood are poor and female; so, to grow up in a generationally poor neighborhood means there is virtually no bridging capital and relatively few men available for bonding capital. Where, then, are your role models? How does a female teach a boy how to interact with other males? Poverty around the world tends to be feminized—whether the cause is war, desertion, death, lack of work, incarceration, or choice.

- **Impediments caused by health issues**—Social development opportunities are further restricted in poverty if you're handicapped physically, are diabetic or obese, have asthma, or are the primary caretaker for the household while the adult works.

- **Absence of support for organized sports**—A primary means of socialization for boys is organized sports. If you're poor, you don't have the financial resources or the support system to participate in them. Participating in organized athletics requires money for equipment, gas for the van, and an adult with time to go with you. If you have only one parent, and that parent is working, who takes you to practice? Who picks you up? As a poor male, you're left unsupervised to develop your social bonds with other male peers. You may play basketball at the park, but you won't have a coach—and your experience will be largely unsupervised. The early experiences that many middle-class males receive being on a T-ball or Little League team, going to professional basketball games, and having good sports equipment are seldom available to those from more impoverished environments. Just as importantly, social bonding with other adult males doesn't occur.

- **Lack of experience with teamwork and cooperation**—Because the typical style of conflict resolution in poverty is zero sum—I win/ you lose—cooperating with a team while competing can be a foreign concept. As a result, violence is a common occurrence when teamwork is required. This has important implications for the world of work: when being tougher than others is critical to survival itself, when one hasn't learned how to cooperate to win, then all relationships and partnerships, including those with colleagues, are seen as competitive (Deutsch, Coleman, & Marcus, 2006; Jordan, 1996).

- **Absence of collective efficacy**—According to a recent report titled "Neighborhoods and the Black-White Mobility Gap" (Sharkey, 2009), the characteristics of a neighborhood greatly impact both the level of violence among males in poverty and the neighborhood's collective efficacy, which is the level of neighborhood responsibility and trust. Berliner (2009) cites a study in which collective efficacy accounted for 75 percent of the variation in violence levels.

- **Scarcity of or inability to work**—Work for males in poor neighborhoods is often intermittent and unstable. In such neighborhoods, it is common to hear the phrase, "I was looking for a job when I found this one." The emphasis is on a job, not a career. As a result, men who work and can provide economic security are rarely seen, and therefore not valued.

- **Devaluation of education**—Another aspect of collective efficacy is the presence of role models, not just in sports, but in the broader social environment. Even when educated male role models are available, the culture of poverty often works against them. Generational poverty doesn't value an educated man. In fact, to be called book smart in poverty is not a compliment. The poverty neighborhood environment values a man who is street smart, a man who can fight and provide physical protection—which has huge value in poverty—and a man who is sexually potent. If you're an adolescent male living in poverty, nobody cares if you get an A in algebra, because in the environment of survival, that doesn't bring any immediate value.

- **Overexposure to television**—Poor households watch more TV (the least expensive form of entertainment) than educated households; along with video games, the TV is often used as a babysitter. Who are the male role models on TV? Typically, they are men who triumph through violence and sexual conquest. Rarely are these role models family men, working men, men coping with the complexities and dilemmas of ordinary life and real relationships.

Supporting the Social Development of Boys

Table 5.1 shows what can be done to provide the kinds of socialization experiences for males that will help them stay engaged in and graduate from high school.

Table 5.1: Supporting Boys' Social Development to Prevent Dropout

Preschool Years (birth to age 4)	Never let children play alone on the playground. Always assign them a buddy.
	Tell stories about how children learn to play together peacefully.
	Use the Storybook to Improve Behavior worksheet (appendix, page 108).
	Avoid the use of DVDs and television in the classroom.
	Educate parents on the effects of television and playing video games.
Boyhood (ages 5–10, kindergarten –grade 5)	Make sure no child eats alone at lunch or plays alone on the playground.
	Make sure team selections and divisions in physical education classes are done in a way that doesn't embarrass or alienate students.
	Have students discuss what they do well and what they contribute to a group.
	Teach the roles needed for a group to function well. Someone needs to be a leader, someone needs to record, someone needs to ask questions, someone needs to encourage others to talk, someone needs to evaluate and comment on the progress toward the goals of the group.
	Prohibit bullying or taunting. Don't confuse playful teasing among boys with bullying. Playful teasing is a way boys have of showing affection to one another.
	Provide structured activities and causes that students can work for as a group.
	Identify media messages and biases.
	Talk with fathers about the importance of coming to school functions (modeling the value of school).
	Invite males to mentor selected boys (role models, potential bridging capital).

continued on next page →

Adolescence (ages 11–16, grades 6–10)	Discuss personal strengths. Assess students' personal resource bases.
	Identify heroes. Whom do students want to be like, and why? How do these heroes make life better for others?
	Teach the roles needed for a group to function well. Someone needs to be a leader, someone needs to record, someone needs to ask questions, someone needs to encourage others to talk, someone needs to evaluate and comment on the progress made toward the goals of the group.
	Prohibit bullying.
	Provide community service activities as a part of the curriculum.
	Have intramural activities.
	Make certain every student is in intramurals, music, band, sports, or a club. Be creative, so that all boys are included in something. One popular offering that draws on interest in media is a film-critics club.
	Identify media messages and biases. Are they true? Are real people like that?
Early Manhood (ages 17–23, grade 11 to post–high school)	Identify community organizations that support the well-being of the community (Rotary, Kiwanis, and Chamber of Commerce, for example).
	Teach the roles needed for a group to function well (leader, encourager, contributor, clarifier, recorder, and summarizer). Someone needs to be a leader, someone needs to record, someone needs to ask questions, someone needs to encourage others to talk, someone needs to evaluate and comment on the progress toward the goals of the group.
	Prohibit bullying.
	Provide community service activities as a part of the curriculum.
	Have intramural activities.
	Make certain every student is in intramurals, music, band, sports, or a club activity.
	Assess students' personal resource bases. Make a plan for developing and building more resources.

6

The Impact of Drugs, Alcohol, and Early Sexual Activity on Boys

In this chapter, we look at the effects of substance abuse, alcohol, and precocious sexuality on boys' development, examine the effect of generational poverty on these issues, and explore ways to support boys in navigating through these potential risks to their education.

The Failure of Drug Education

Alcohol and drugs are problems in schools, and students know it. In 2008, a national sampling of teens was asked to identify the most important problem "kids your age face." Of the respondents, 28 percent cited substance issues (19 percent specified drugs, 7 percent alcohol, and 1 percent tobacco). Another 1 percent cited drinking and driving (National Center on Addiction and Substance Abuse, 2008).

Unfortunately, drug education programs in schools in the United States have largely been a failure. In 2002, the government acknowledged that its $900 million, five-year ad campaign designed to discourage drug use wasn't working. Drugs, alcohol, and sex are still readily available to most teens. One reason for the program's failure is that girls and boys who engage in drug use do so for very different reasons, and so a one-size-fits-all drug education program doesn't actually fit all. For girls, drug use is usually connected to low self-esteem, and girls are more likely to get drugs from a friend. Girls will take pills that help them lose weight, give them more energy, or become more personable or funny. They have a need to fit in with certain groups, to be accepted by a group, or to be popular with boys. The lower her self-esteem, the more likely a girl will experiment with drugs (Donovan, 1996; Kumpulainen & Roine, 2002; National Center on Addiction and Substance Abuse, 2003).

For boys, it's a very different story. According to Geoffrey Canada (1998), boys who are risk takers and thrill seekers are much more prone to engage in drug use than boys who aren't. Drug use is "a feeling of power, of being kind of indestructible," said one recovering teen (Kindlon & Thompson, 2000, p. 180). These males, even as young boys, show no fear and engage in activities in which they might get hurt. They are convinced they can experiment with drugs and not get hooked on them.

Here are some sobering statistics about drug and marijuana use in the United States:

- More than 30 percent of tenth-grade boys report having smoked marijuana during the year previous to the study, and nearly 40 percent of male high school seniors smoked pot within the same year (Kindlon & Thompson, 2000).

- Seven percent of teenage boys smoke pot every day (Kindlon & Thompson, 2000).

- Twenty-three percent of teens (5.8 million) are able to obtain marijuana in an hour or less, and 42 percent (10.6 million) are able to get it in a day or less. As teens get older, their access to marijuana increases. Forty-three percent of the seventeen-year-olds surveyed can get marijuana in an hour or less, compared with only 6 percent of twelve-year-olds (National Center on Addiction and Substance Abuse, 2008).

- Fourteen percent of male high school students have tried LSD; 7 percent have tried cocaine (Kindlon & Thompson, 2000).

- Drug use rates in the senior year of high school tend to be at least 1.5 to 2.5 times higher among boys than girls (Kindlon & Thompson, 2000).

- A national survey conducted between 2007 and 2008 found a 46 percent increase in teens' use of prescription drugs (National Center on Addiction and Substance Abuse, 2008).

- In 2008, for the first time, teens said that prescription drugs are easier to obtain than beer (National Center on Addiction and Substance Abuse, 2008).

- Twenty-four percent of teens have friends who abuse prescription drugs. While 10 percent of the twelve-year-olds surveyed say they have a friend or classmate who abuses prescription drugs, nearly half of the seventeen-year-olds (47 percent) say they have one or more friends who abuse prescription drugs (National Center on Addiction and Substance Abuse, 2008).

- One-third of teens say their sources for prescription drugs are friends or classmates. Another one-third say they get prescription drugs from home—either from the medicine cabinet or from their parents. Only 9 percent say they get prescription drugs from a drug dealer (National Center on Addiction and Substance Abuse, 2008).

- Nearly half the respondents say painkillers are the most popular class of prescription drugs among teens their age (National Center on Addiction and Substance Abuse, 2008).

Alcohol's Effects on Boys

Alcohol compromises learning, memory, abstract thinking, problem solving, attention, and concentration (Office of Applied Studies, 2008). It is no wonder, then, that early alcohol use is associated with increased likelihood of unprotected sexual intercourse and multiple sex partners (Stueve & O'Donnell, 2005; Swahn, Bossarte, & Sullivent, 2008). Alcohol is also an analgesic (painkiller) that strongly affects the brain's endogenous opiate system, the part of the brain that produces natural painkiller (Froehlich, 1997). Is it any surprise that many boys and young men use alcohol as an escape?

When boys drink, they almost always drink to excess. That is why, for adolescent boys, any drinking is problem drinking. Alcohol consumption is the cause as well as the effect of reckless behavior in boys. With heavy drinking comes high-risk behavior (Kindlon & Thompson, 2000).

Longitudinal studies consistently suggest that exposure to alcohol advertising and promotion increases the likelihood that adolescents will start to use alcohol or will drink more if they're already drinking (Anderson, de Bruijn, Angus, Gordon, & Hastings, 2009). The statistics regarding alcohol use among boys in the United States show the following:

- Of current drinkers ages twelve to seventeen, fully 31 percent had extreme levels of psychological distress, and 39 percent had serious behavioral problems. Adolescents who drink heavily are 3 to 4 times more likely to attempt suicide. The average boy takes his first drink at age eleven, the average girl at age thirteen (Office of Applied Studies, 2008).

- Boys who drink are prone to fighting and sexual aggression. One study suggests that males are almost twice as likely as females to engage in alcohol-related physical fighting (Office of Applied Studies, 2008).

- Among high school males, 39 percent say it's acceptable for a boy to force a girl who is drunk or high to have sex (Office of Applied Studies, 2008).

- Researchers estimate that alcohol use is implicated in one third to two thirds of sexual assault and date rape cases among teens and college students (Office of Applied Studies, 2008).

- A 2006 study concluded that nearly one in five persons between the ages of eighteen and twenty drove under the influence of alcohol (Office of Applied Studies, 2007).

- Each year approximately 1,900 people under the age of twenty-one die because of motor vehicle crashes in which alcohol was involved (Hingson & Kenkel, 2004).

Early Sexual Activity

A *New York Times* article (Jarrell, 2000) reported that "young people are engaging in sex at younger and younger ages. Besides intercourse, they are engaging in oral sex, mutual masturbation, nudity, and exposure as precursors to intercourse."

The same article commented on the mixed messages that young people receive today about sexuality:

> On the one hand, bombarded by warnings about AIDS and sexually transmitted diseases, adolescents are taught abstinence, the sole contraception method taught at one-third of all public schools across the country, according to a poll by the Alan Guttmacher Institute, a private research organization. On the other hand, teenagers are confronted daily with a culture that has become a very sexy place indeed in which to live. "Sex is everywhere, and it's absolutely explicit," said Allen Waltzman, a psychiatrist. . . . "There's hardly a film that doesn't show a man and a woman having sex. There's MTV, lurid rap lyrics, and now we've got technosex on the Internet."

The exposure of even young children to images of explicit sex in the media and to sensual advertising has created a sexually active, sexual thrill-seeking population in high schools. Young children today watch commercials that address everything from erectile dysfunction to sanitary napkins to breast augmentation. They watch movies in which people have sex on first dates or with someone they just happened to meet in a bar. The days when a teenage boy knocked on the door and met the girl's parents prior to a date are mostly a thing of the past. The ritual has changed to a casual, impersonal sexual encounter with no strings attached—often simply termed *hooking up*.

Jarrell (2000) reports that Frederick Kaeser, director of health services for District 2 of the New York public school system, sees younger displays of not only "precocious sexual behavior but also aggressive molestation" at younger ages. Jarrell related the following story of a boy of thirteen from New York. His interest in sex began in third grade, when he started watching *Beverly Hills 90210*, a television show about teenagers from affluent families. The thirteen-year-old said, "The people were cool. I wanted to try what they were doing on the show." By third grade, he and his male friends knew the slang words for masturbation and oral sex. By fourth grade, they had girlfriends and were playing kissing games. By fifth grade, they were going on dates. In sixth grade, they were French kissing and petting. In seventh and eighth grades they were trying oral sex, and some had intercourse. Role identification with a television show was key in this situation. For boys in poverty, there are numerous such examples of sexual activity and violence in movies and television shows.

Sax (2005) comments on a *Newsweek* report that between 1991 and 2001 the percentage of high school seniors who reported they had had sexual intercourse decreased from 54 to 46 percent. Upon investigating the data more closely; however, researchers discovered there had simply been a drop in penile-vaginal intercourse. The "in" thing is now oral sex, with boys and girls hooking up at a party at someone's house. Smoking marijuana is also frequently part of the encounter.

Psychiatrists and psychologists report that young people in our society are not developmentally equipped to handle the emotions that go with early sex. Quoting again from Jarrell (2000):

> Levy-Warren said, "They're trying to figure out who they are, and unlike adults who obsess first and then act, kids do the opposite—they act and then obsess. What is most troubling . . . is a new casual, brazen attitude about sex. I call it body-part sex. The kids don't even look at each other. It's mechanical, dehumanizing. The fallout is that later in life they have trouble forming relationships. They're jaded."

For many boys, sex is an urge that has its own agenda; it isn't about relationships. For girls, a fulfilling sexual experience has, traditionally, been more likely to occur when it's part of a meaningful relationship. What has changed over time is that many girls have essentially adopted the boys' view of sex. The boy no longer has to declare that he's in love with the girl to get sex. The old adage that "boys use love to get sex, while girls use sex to find love" is becoming obsolete. Hooking up has replaced relationships.

The use of drugs and alcohol often accompanies sex and can further rob the sexual experience of intimacy and emotional connection. Drew Pinsky made the following comment as a guest on Terry Gross's National Public Radio program, *Fresh Air*:

> Both girls and boys are usually partly drunk or totally drunk when they hook up. . . . Girls and boys give completely different reasons why they get drunk before they hook up. Boys like to get drunk because it slows down their sexual response, allows them to relax, and decreases the likelihood of premature ejaculation. Girls like to get drunk because it numbs the experience for them, making it less embarrassing and less emotionally painful. (Gross & Miller, 2003)

Emotional Consequences

The harm of early sexual experience for girls is obvious—the risk of pregnancy—along with a devalued sense of the sacred that could jade them. What most people don't talk about is the consequence for boys. Although many dads look the other way when they discover their son is sexually active, and some even display pride in their son's conquests, when boys are sexually active and engage in sex that is disconnected from intimacy, they do not develop the emotional connectedness that is needed for later adult relationships. Sax (2005) describes the harm done to boys as follows:

> By the time a heterosexual young man is in his early twenties, he will rely on his girlfriend or his wife to be his primary emotional caregiver. And the reliance only becomes greater as he moves through adult life. Straight men who don't have a wife or girlfriend are substantially more likely to become seriously depressed, commit suicide, or die from illness. (p. 131)

While most girls and women have a support system that includes their mom and sisters, coworkers, and girlfriends (Campbell & Lee, 1992; Fischer & Oliker, 1983; Moore, 1990), friendships among males are often based on shared activities and interests. Boys and men don't necessarily share their innermost feelings with male friends.

The Role of Sports

Soccer, basketball, softball, and swim teams are excellent avenues for help-ing girls feel good about themselves. A girl's appearance is not much of an issue in these sports. They don't require being pretty, as do being a cheerleader or drill team member. The National Center on Addiction and Substance Abuse (2008) found that girls who participated in three or more extracurricular ac-tivities during the school year are only half as likely to smoke cigarettes, drink alcohol, or use marijuana.

For boys, however, competitive sports are not necessarily a deterrent to substance abuse. Playing sports doesn't decrease a boy's interest in thrill seek-ing or wanting to look cool. Boys who are risk takers are sometimes the most active and best athletes. Boys tend to obtain their drugs from total strangers—that, in and of itself, is a thrill-seeking event ("Can I purchase the drug and not get caught?").

Thrill-seeking boys will attempt to ski down a mountain without a lesson or refuse to wear a helmet while riding a Harley. Parents of these boys have to establish very tight parameters for them, and the punishment must be a conse-quence that the boy feels is real punishment, such as, "If I catch you drinking, you lose all driving privileges for six months." A teenage boy wants his in-dependence and mobility. Lock up the video games and PlayStation while grounding him for three months. Get the thrill-seeking boys involved in safer activities that fulfill some of that need for a thrill: encourage mountain climb-ing, dirt-bike riding, skateboard competitions, and so on. A broken bone is much better than a needle in the arm.

Boys in poverty are more likely to grow up in a risk-taking environment. Structuring risk taking activities for these boys is more difficult. In some neigh-borhoods, daily activities of going to school or walking to the store may be a risk. Boys & Girls Clubs of America, YMCA, and Boy Scouts may provide some options for these boys.

Dinner Together: A Key Intervention

Study after study has identified one intervention that seems to work for both boys and girls: children in families who eat dinner together are much less likely to abuse drugs, have sex, or drink alcohol (Griffin, Botvin, Scheier, Diaz, & Miller, 2000; National Center on Addiction and Substance Abuse, 2009; Sax, 2005). The hours between four o'clock and seven o'clock, after school but be-fore parents get home from work, are often the hours for experimentation. For those boys and girls who don't have after-school activities, a parent can assign chores, such as setting the table or starting to prepare dinner. A parent can request, "Peel the potatoes before I get home, and make the salad" or "Please make the spaghetti." Having dinner together should be a high priority for parents, and it should be non-negotiable for their sons and daughters. Dinnertime—with the television turned off—is the time to talk about friends, what's happening at school and work, what everyone watched on TV last night, plans for the weekend, and so on.

Generational Poverty and Drugs, Alcohol, and Early Sexual Activity

Generational poverty exacerbates boys' problems with substance abuse, alcohol, and premature sexual activity in the following ways:

- **Lack of adult supervision**—Because many children in poverty have a single parent who often works two jobs, adult supervision tends to be limited. If the parent also has mental health or drug addiction issues—or is in a domestic violence situation, in prison, physically handicapped, or absent, then there's even less supervision. For children in these families, interventions like eating dinner together in the evening as a family are usually not even an option.

- **Absence of males**—Criminologists can predict the level of violence in neighborhoods with a remarkable degree of accuracy using two factors: the educational attainment level of the adults and the number of households that do not have men living in them on a permanent basis.

- **Fatalistic attitudes**—In poverty, there's a strong belief in fate. It is not uncommon, in poor neighborhoods, to hear, "When it's your time to die, it's your time to die." When we asked an eighteen-year-old in poverty what his life would be like when he was twenty-five years old, he told us he would never reach twenty-five. Gang initiation, getting beat up or shot on the way home from school, holding your own in a fight, facing down the bully—these are risks faced by boys growing up in generational poverty. If you believe you're going to die young, your behaviors don't matter very much. The key issues of concern are when you're going to die and not getting caught before you do.

- **Premature exposure to sexuality**—Sex isn't much of a secret in generational poverty. Because more people occupy less space, privacy is a luxury, and sexual activity can be heard, smelled, and often seen. Early initiation into sexual activity is also not uncommon. Vincent

Ianelli (2010) found that "children whose parents are unemployed have about two times the rate of child abuse and two to three times the rate of neglect than children with employed parents. Children in low socioeconomic families have more than three times the rate of child abuse and seven times the rate of neglect than other children."

- **Overvaluation of sexual experience**—Having sex in generational poverty is a primary rite of passage, something you must do to be considered an adult by your peer group. In middle-class life, a rite of passage is getting a driver's license, a high school diploma, or a job. In wealth, it's about getting interest from your trust fund, then eventually controlling your trust fund. In poverty, fathering or mothering a child is often the visible sign that you are a "real" man or woman.

To make matters worse, in poverty, the resources necessary to prevent pregnancy, even if the partners want to, generally aren't readily available. Condoms, birth control pills, intrauterine devices, and other birth control measures usually cost money that isn't available. In fact, the increase in oral and anal sex (Sax, 2005) may be attributed, in part, to a desire to prevent pregnancy while still having sex.

- **Easy availability of drugs and alcohol**—There is great debate in the field of mental health about which comes first—the biochemical issue that needs to be addressed or the addiction, which eventually creates a biochemical issue. Setting aside causation, in poverty, drugs, alcohol, and tobacco are virtually always present and readily available—if not in the home, then in the neighborhood. Resources generally aren't available to address this issue, so it becomes a daily reality. Moreover, in generational poverty, the definition of a real man includes the ability to hold his liquor, making alcohol consumption something to be proud of. While drugs, alcohol, and addiction are present in middle class and wealth as well, those socioeconomic groups have more resources available to confront the problem and mitigate some of the damage.

Protecting Boys from Drugs, Alcohol, and Early Sexual Activity

Table 6.1 (page 72) shows what can be done to protect boys from drugs and alcohol and decrease precocious sexual experiences, with the goal of helping them remain engaged in school.

Table 6.1: Protecting Boys From Drugs, Alcohol, and Early Sexual Activity

Preschool Years (birth to age 4)	Provide interactions with healthy adult males. If no father is available, involve appropriate men in religious settings, in school, among relatives, and so on. Special education needs to network with hospitals and local clinics for early identification of students with special needs, particularly those with chemical dependency, so that early intervention can be planned.
Boyhood (ages 5–10, kindergarten –grade 5)	Provide after-school clubs from 4 to 7 p.m. that provide supervision to boys. Help students complete the Future Story exercise (page 109). Provide opportunities for job shadowing. Use relational learning.
Adolescence (ages 11–16, grades 6–10)	Encourage clubs where boys spend time with male mentors. Meet with a group of boys periodically on a Saturday to shoot hoops. Locate sponsors or donations for field trips to a basketball game, a museum, a university, a theatrical performance, skate boarding clubs, dirt bike riding, mountain climbing, hiking, surfboards, karate, team sports, and so on. Help students complete the Future Story exercise (page 109). Provide opportunities for job shadowing. Use relational learning. Have students complete a self-assessment using the Personal Resource Assessments (page 101). Complete a Graduation Plan (page 110).
Early Manhood (ages 17–23, grade 11 to post–high school)	Help students become email buddies with successful male adults. Encourage students to enroll with a buddy in a local community college class. Assess student aptitude to assist in career selection. Read Tom Rath's *Strengthsfinder 2.0* (2007). Have students complete the Personal Resource Assessments (page 101). Help students to complete the Future Story exercise (page 109).

7

The Different Boy: Sensitive, Gay, Gifted, ADHD

Learning what it's like to be a man is a difficult journey even for boys with wonderful, supportive families who have the resources necessary to provide the physical and emotional support they need to become responsible, caring adults. For boys who are packaged a little differently, that journey can be overwhelming, leaving them feeling despair and shame and unable to develop feelings of self-worth, confidence, and pride. Although any one of these hurdles is huge, when they're combined in one individual, the effect can be catastrophic academically, socially, physically, and emotionally. This chapter focuses on some of those overwhelming challenges, how they are exacerbated by generational poverty, and what interventions we can use to mitigate their effect on boys' experience of education.

Sensitive Boys

Sensitive boys are boys who typically do well in school but do not fit into the typical male world. For example, they may have little or no athletic ability but may be artistic, attuned to the feelings of others, and more comfortable in the company of girls than boys. Sensitive boys are vulnerable. They are sometimes the butt of jokes, teasing, and taunting by other boys (Paymar, 2000). Sometimes they are verbally ridiculed, called names, excluded from groups, and left isolated with their feelings of despair. Young and Sweeting (2004) found that "gender atypical" boys were victimized and lonely, had fewer male friends, and experienced greater psychological distress than "gender typical" boys (Swearer, Turner, Givens, & Pollack, 2008). S. J. Bergman (2003) says it this way:

It can begin with being teased for playing a girls' game or for being "chicken,"
and it becomes the companion of every soldier who, facing battle, dreads
his own terror and the possibility that his unmanly fear will cause him to
act like a coward. Boy culture is competitive, insensitive, and often cruel.
Being chosen last, or not at all, is a vivid memory for most men. Being
picked on, afraid to fight, or forced to fight generates a welter of intense
feelings, with shame at the core. (p. 93)

The interests of sensitive boys are also different from those of other boys
(Newman, Woodcock, & Dunham, 2006). They may not be interested in or
good at sports (Kimmel, 2005; Kimmel & Aronson, 2003). Instead, they may
be interested in art, music, literature, or dance. Boys who are interested in
the arts may find themselves teased, labeled as gay, and avoided by other boys
(Sax, 2007).

Sensitive boys are usually empathic and may show a concern for those less
fortunate or social issues (Gurian & Stevens, 2005; Howell, 2002; Pollack, 1998).
They typically have mothers who are very protective and fathers who are somewhat removed—who neither understand nor respect their sons. Dad may be a
"macho" kind of father. Where does the sensitive boy learn how to be a man
if he doesn't have many of the interests that most boys and men seem to have?

Added to all this, some boys—and girls—assume that a boy who is different
is gay. Rivers, Duncan, and Besag (2007) reported that over 1.6 million public
school students, are bullied each year because of their actual or perceived sexual orientation. (Swearer, et al., 2008). Young people find it distressing to be
harassed based on perceived sexual orientation (American Association of University Women Educational Foundation, 1993; Swearer et al., 2008). Whether
a boy is gay or not, the assumption that he is adds yet another obstacle with
which he must deal.

During adolescence, sensitive boys are frequently alone and often lack
self-confidence. At this stage of development, social isolation can be a pro-
foundly painful emotional experience. Adolescents who report having no
close friendships consistently have lower levels of self-esteem and exhibit more
psychological symptoms of maladjustment (Berndt, Hawkins, & Jaio, 1999;
Stocker, 1994). With overly protective mothers, sensitive males usually lag behind other boys in social maturity, remaining younger emotionally and socially
than their chronological years.

Kimmel and Mahler (2003) found that in nearly all accounts of random
school shootings from 1982 to 2001, the shooters (all male) reported having
been harassed "for inadequate gender performance" (p. 1440). "The shooters
were not victimized because they were actually gay," the authors clarify, "but

rather because they were 'different from other boys—shy, bookish, honor students, artistic, musical, theatrical, nonathletic, 'geekish,' or weird'" (p. 1445). Noting the geographic locations of these events—primarily white, middle-class, rural, or suburban schools, not inner cities that are generally more associated with violence—Kimmel and Mahler suggest that attitudes toward gender nonconformity, particularly for boys, becomes a foundation for bullying and, ultimately in a few tragic cases, for lethal school violence (Swearer et al., 2008). Ryan Lee (2005), in looking at masculinity issues as they have contributed to fatal school shootings, states: "No weapon is more emasculating or brandished more frequently on schoolyards across the country, than homophobic rhetoric used to describe anything that makes a young man different from his male peers." Lee cites Michael Kimmel and Matthew Mahler's June 2003 article for *American Behavioral Scientist*, in which they wrote, "We found a striking pattern [while analyzing news] stories about the boys who committed the violence: nearly all had stories of being constantly bullied, beat up, and 'gay-baited.'"

Gay Boys

Boys who are gay tend to feel even more poignantly the isolation that comes with being outside the norm: "Stigma is social shame, the shame of membership in a scorned group. . . . It exerts a profound influence on . . . gay men" (Levant & Pollack, 2003, p. 115). Students today may show a greater tolerance for gay youths than they did fifteen or twenty years ago, but these boys still face enormous obstacles. Homophobia is prevalent almost everywhere. All too often, male teens in high school who appear to others to be gay endure ridicule, social isolation, and alienation. Dances and other social events may be awkward, and gay males are often threatened with violence, verbal harassment, and social ostracism (Goldstein & Goldstein, 2000). According to data from a Human Rights Watch study (as cited in Swearer et al., 2008), gay, lesbian, bisexual, and transgendered youths are:

- Nearly three times as likely as their heterosexual peers to have been assaulted or involved in at least one physical fight in school

- Three times as likely to have been threatened or injured with a weapon at school

- Nearly four times as likely to have skipped school because they felt unsafe

Being gay isn't the only sexual difference that some boys wrestle with. A *transsexual* is someone born as a male who self-identifies as a female, or someone born female who self-identifies as a male (Griggs, 1998; Hausman,

1995). These individuals feel trapped in the wrong body. A *transvestite* is someone who finds it sexually arousing to dress as the opposite gender (Bullough &
Bullough, 1993). A male transvestite identifies with female stereotypes in such
things as clothing, hair, makeup, shopping, and other female interests (Ekins &
King, 1996; Herman-Jeglinska, Grabowska, & Dulko, 2002; Lawrence, 2003).

Boys like these who are different often feel shame. When boys experience
all—or even most—of these differences, it can be overwhelming for both them
and for their parents. Often they are subject to violence based on their sexuality. Support systems are crucial for these boys. They need relationships and
role models to develop their own definitions of manhood. They need validation of their self-worth, of who they are, as they are.

Pilkington and D'Augelli (as cited in Swearer et al., 2008) found that 30
percent of males reported having been harassed or verbally abused in school because of their sexual orientation. Twenty-two percent of the males in the study
reported having been physically hurt. A study involving 500 gay and lesbian
adolescents found that 41 percent had experienced violence, and 46 percent of
that violence was reported as being gay-related (Russell, Franz, & Driscoll,
2001). In a study involving more than nine thousand ninth- through twelfth-
graders, 24 percent of gay or bisexual males reported at-school victimization
ten or more times per year, compared with 2.7 percent of their heterosexual
counterparts (Bontempo & D'Augelli, 2002).

Based on interviews with hundreds of gay boys and men, there appear to
be four key factors that determine the degree to which a young gay boy develops emotional stability:

1　Parental acceptance, especially from fathers

2　Religion or spirituality

3　Community acceptance (including school community)

4　Tolerance within workplace

Young men who aren't accepted by their parents, their family of faith, their
community, and their workplace frequently use drugs and alcohol, are depressed, engage in promiscuity, and are suicidal (Johnson & Johnson, 2000;
Kitts, 2005).

Parental Acceptance

Some parents may suspect their son is gay very early in life; others may remain clueless until the young man comes out to his parents. Until that turning
point, parents may notice their son is a little different. He may prefer being
with girls rather than boys. He may or may not like sports. He may or may

not appear more effeminate than other boys his age. Regardless of how the boy is "packaged," parental acceptance is crucial. The unconditional love that all children need and want is necessary for any boy who sees himself as different (Cochran, Stewart, Ginzler, & Cauce, 2002; D'Augelli, Hershberger, & Pilkington, 1998; Goldfried, 2001; Kitts, 2005; Nelson, 1997).

One man told us in vivid detail an early memory of telling his father when they were in a toy store that he wanted to buy a paper-doll kit. His father replied that he could buy a truck, but if he chose to buy the paper dolls, he would spank him when he got home. The boy selected the paper dolls—and got spanked. For a boy to realize he doesn't meet his father's approval leaves a lasting imprint, one that lasts a lifetime.

A woman we know had a sixteen-year-old son who came out to his friends before he told his parents. His mother finally asked him one day, "Are you gay?"

He said, "Yes, Mom, and thank you for asking. I was trying to find a way to tell you."

Then the mother asked her son, "How do you know?"

"How do you know you're heterosexual?" he asked. "You just know. But I'm worried about what Dad will say."

The mother said, "I love you. I will always love you. Your father loves you, too."

The mother told the father, who visibly paled but said nothing. A week later, the father said to her, "You know, it doesn't change anything. I still love him. He is still the wonderful human being he has always been."

The mother told us that she talked to a colleague who was a lesbian about her son's announcement that he was gay. The mother was very worried about the drugs, AIDS, and violence that plague the gay community. The colleague responded, "There are violence, AIDS, and drugs in the heterosexual community. There are date rape and disease and cocaine. Your son will never need to participate in that community because you are allowing him to be open about who *he* is. The individuals who *need* to operate in that underground community are the ones who cannot be open about who they are."

During his junior year of high school, in an advanced math class, one of this young man's classmates, who had been one of his best friends in middle school, refused to trade papers with him for grading. The classmate said out loud to the whole class—"Yuck. Gay germs. I don't want to touch it." When the young man was a senior, he did not put in his college application biography that he was gay. When his mother asked him why, he said to her, "Being gay is a part of me, but it does not define me. Do you put in your biography that you are heterosexual?"

The mother also told us she had purchased and read every book she could find on being gay so that she could keep her relationship with her son.

Male homosexuality has a biological base; today, there is proof of a genetic factor in some cases (LeVay & Hamer, 1994; Swaminathan, 2008) (though the nature/nurture causation question is still the subject of considerable debate). The genetic factor, however, is subtle. Sax (2005) explains this subtlety with an analogy to being left-handed versus right-handed. We know today that left-handedness is genetically wired. The technology to detect left-handedness in the brain currently doesn't exist, but that doesn't mean it isn't there. The same is true of homosexuality. Observes Sax:

> The differences between the brains of straight men and gay men—whatever those differences may be—are likely to be on orders of magnitude more subtle than the differences between women and men, or between girls and boys. Anatomic differences in the brain based on gender are easily demonstrated. Anatomic differences in the brain based on sexual orientation are—with current technology—too small to be reliably detected. (p. 208)

William Masters and Virginia Johnson (1979) did an extensive study of homosexuality. They found that gay men often engage in sex just for the sake of sex. That didn't prove true of lesbian women, whom they found typically develop a relationship with another woman before engaging in sex. Gay men, they found, also may have anonymous sex. That, also, isn't true of most lesbian women. Does that make gay men different from straight men? Probably not. There are straight men who hire prostitutes; women typically don't do that. Straight men may have casual sex or one-night stands. As discussed in an earlier chapter, many teenage boys today engage in hooking up rather than dating and developing a relationship, and the disengagement from a relationship may say more about the male gender than it does about being gay. The issue for gay boys is that any aspect of oneself that is felt to be shameful or unacceptable tends to break relationships or feelings of intimacy. If I avoid the relationship, I avoid the possible rejection. If that behavior is layered with poverty, then the shame factor is increased. Since poverty puts a strong emphasis on personal strength (you have to have it to survive), anything that is viewed as less manly is a perceived weakness and therefore needs to be negated or refuted.

Religion, Community, and the Workplace

Boys who are raised in religions that teach being gay is a sin usually experience intense shame (Goodwill, 2000). If they attend school or live in a community that isn't "gay friendly," they feel they must hide their sexuality (Lipkin, 1999; Sandoval, 2002). As gay men enter the workplace, they also may be subjected to ridicule and be the brunt of jokes—or even the objects of gay bashing (Kantor, 1998). Gay police officers, firefighters, and sports figures frequently experience such remarks (Swan & Dekker, 2004). One theory about why there appear to be so few gay sports figures is that they would limit their potential product endorsement revenue if they were to come out. The "don't ask, don't tell" policy in the United States armed forces, which communicates that a soldier can be courageous and die for his country, but he just can't be courageous and *gay* and die for his country, has caused many young men to hide their sexuality (Belkin & Bateman, 2003; Estes, 2005).

Progress has been made since 2000. Gay rights have certainly achieved more public attention, with an increasing number of states currently legalizing civil unions of same-sex partners. Workplaces have formed support systems for their gay and lesbian employees. Some urban schools have allowed gay and lesbian student groups to meet. More parents have been more outspoken and supportive of their sons and daughters in school, demanding safe environments for their children. However, rural areas, small towns, more conservative parts of the country, and certain religious groups have not necessarily seen these improvements, and young men from those environments often feel very isolated and misunderstood. Parents of boys in poverty typically do not go to school and advocate for them. Furthermore, the discussions about sexual orientation generally are limited. When you are at survival, that kind of discussion is a luxury.

Gifted Boys

A gifted boy doesn't experience many of his problems until he enters adolescence. By the time many gifted boys have reached middle school, they've been labeled geeks and nerds, and they frequently find themselves excluded from guy groups. It is rare for highly gifted children to escape the effects of their differences from age-group peers. The risk of social isolation, inappropriate educational response, and a lack of authentic interaction is particularly troublesome (Jackson, 1995, as cited in Jackson & Peterson, 2003).

The embarrassment, even humiliation, that gifted children experience by being so labeled causes many boys to underachieve and even withdraw from gifted programs. If they're Hispanic or African American, they may feel even greater dismay and discomfort, because they're smart (Ford, 1995, 1996; Ford, Harris, & Schuerger, 1993; Fordham, 1988; Fordham & Ogbu, 1986; Lindstrom & Van Sant, 1986; VanTassel-Baska, 1989; Whitmore, 1980). According to James Moore, Donna Ford, and Richard Milner (2005, p. 4):

Unfortunately, African American and Hispanic students seem particularly susceptible to negative opposition from their peers (Ogbu, 2003; Shaffer et al., 2002). These students, especially in urban settings, are frequently teased by their peer groups as acting white when they appear to be academically engaged (Corwin, 2001; Fordham, 1988; Suskind, 1998).

If they're from poverty, it becomes even more intense, because in poverty, it's especially not cool to be smart. Consider Matt Damon's character in the movie *Good Will Hunting*. Damon plays a mathematical genius who comes from a background of physical abuse and poverty. A teacher we knew had a ninth-grade boy from poverty in class who was very smart, yet was deliberately failing. Finally, the teacher took him aside and asked him to explain. He finally exploded and said, "If I get an A, I won't have any friends!" They compromised on a C.

Some gifted boys who try to live up to their perceptions of giftedness also may experience feelings of great inadequacy, believing, "If I'm so gifted, why can't I do X well?" As girls have entered more courses and lines of work that traditionally were male dominated, males have abandoned many of those areas, leaving women in the majority. This is resulting in more and more bright males with fewer options. In *Smart Boys*, Barbara Kerr and Sanford Cohn (2001) comment:

> In the world of work, it has long been observed that when women enter any occupation in great numbers, the status and salary of that occupation go down, and this is not due simply to an influx of additional persons in the occupation. Therefore, "male flight" is probably very similar to "white flight," because they fear that the entry of too many of another group will make "property values" go down. (p. 95)

In poverty, the environment rewards physical process. Educated households understand that the pen is mightier than the sword. But in poverty, the sword is concrete, strong, and understood. Words from a pen are not respected or seen as a strength. Therefore, to be "gifted" in poverty means you are not understood. You are weird. What do you talk about that interests both you and others? Therefore, you are ostracized and emotionally, mentally, and sometimes physically isolated. It is also often difficult in poverty to find educated adults who have mutual interests.

ADHD Boys

A 2004 study found that boys in general, as well as children born to parents who have low education levels, are at an increased risk for developing ADHD (attention deficit hyperactivity disorder) compared with girls and children born to parents with high levels of education (Medical News Today, 2004). Kerr & Cohen (2001) say, referring to ADHD, that "usually by fourth or fifth grade, the boy's 'disability' will manifest itself as underachievement and gross disorganization" (p. 111).

However, there appears to be an overuse of this diagnosis, which results in many gifted boys being medicated (Worrell, 2001). Hyperactivity, inattention, and impulsivity are all normal behaviors of boys. It's the degree to which boys manifest those traits that makes them ADHD. Gifted boys usually have a high activity level, and many end up labeled as ADHD or ADD (attention deficit disorder) (Kerr & Cohn, 2001; Webb, Amend, & Webb, 2006). Boys from poverty may also be labeled ADHD because of their impulsivity. When boys are placed in a boy-friendly classroom, however, they're much less likely to be labeled ADHD than if they're placed in a rigid, come-in, sit-down, and get-to-work classroom.

The medications that boys who are labeled as ADHD take can be problematic. Boys who are medicated may experience side effects of the drug. Studies have demonstrated that many boys who are medicated end up later in life on two or three drugs to deal with some of these side effects (Sax, 2007). Moreover, it's difficult to assess the effectiveness or use of medication for ADHD—particularly in extreme poverty. First of all, access to a professional to diagnose the issue is limited. Medication costs money. If they do get the medication, it is not unusual in poverty for adults or students to sell it for the money. A psychologist in Minnesota told us that whenever he prescribed Ritalin for a child, the adults would take the medicine and use it themselves. Furthermore, disorganization is often common in poverty, so it is not viewed as an issue or problem. People living in poverty tend to be reactive rather than proactive.

There is concern among many professionals that Ritalin is overprescribed, especially for boys, before the problem has been fully evaluated. "Sometimes a child is inattentive, impulsive, or hyperactive for reasons that have nothing to do with ADHD" (Saks, 2007, p. 196). In 2003, *USA Today* reported that there were then more than four million boys taking Ritalin in the United States (Girls Get Extra School Help, 2003). That doesn't count other drugs that are being prescribed for them by physicians:

> Instead of pursuing sound solutions, many educators merely advocate prescribing more attention-focusing Ritalin for the boys, who receive the drug at four to eight times the rate of girls, according to different estimates. "Too often the first reaction to an attention problem is 'Let's medicate,'" says Rockville, Md., child psychologist Neil Hoffman. "Some

schools are quick to recommend solutions before they've fully evaluated the problem."

When a teacher suggests to parents that they may want to get their son evaluated for ADHD, the parents usually go to the family physician, but the family doctor is not the person who can officially diagnose a boy as ADHD. This diagnosis should be made by a psychologist. The psychologist, however, can't prescribe medication; only a physician can. To complicate matters, insurance companies often won't pay for the diagnostic work of a psychologist, but they will pay for the doctor's office visit. The result? The physician prescribes Ritalin and asks the parents to come back in six weeks, saying, "We'll see if it makes a difference." Six weeks later the parents take the child back and report that he seems to be doing better. The conclusion: he must have ADHD. However, while Ritalin is designed to increase a person's ability to concentrate and focus, being able to concentrate and focus while taking the drug isn't proof that a boy has ADHD.

Generational Poverty and Sensitive, Gay, Gifted, and ADHD Boys

Generational poverty can exacerbate the situation of boys who are sensitive; gay, gifted, or ADHD in the following ways:

- **Lack of discussion of difficult issues**—As we have seen, in poverty, the language to discuss things tends to be limited. Being gay, gifted, or sensitive is often hidden or not explored, with conflicts left to fester.

- **Rigidity of definitions of maleness**—The bias against sensitive and gay men leads to prejudices against intelligence and giftedness; failure in school becomes proof you aren't smart. In poverty, giftedness is okay if it isn't about academic pursuits. To be "gifted" in athletics, music, or acting is admired because it is a "concrete" world of physical prowess. However, to be gay or sensitive in the culture of generational poverty is not to be male. Males are frequently pushed into heterosexual relationships as proof that they aren't gay.

- **Lack of health care**—The availability of medication for ADHD in poverty has two extremes: either the drug is actively sought on the black market, or the money and resources to purchase it legally are not available. Sometimes, even when it's available, medication in poverty is sold to take care of other expenses.

- **Overprescription of stimulant medications**—Sax (2007, p. 199), who is both an MD and PhD, recommends the following:

> Avoid the use of stimulant medications: Adderall, Ritalin, Concerta, Metadate, Focalin, Daytrana, and their generic equivalents, amphetamine and methylphenidate. . . . The lower the dose . . . of stimulant medications, the lower the risk of toxicity. . . . [They] pose a risk to the brain that Strattera and Wellbutrin do not pose. . . . The boy with true ADHD who needs 30 mg of Adderall everyday to function well at school will often do just as well with 25 mg of Strattera and 5 mg of Adderall.

Supporting Boys Who Are Sensitive, Gay, Gifted, and ADHD

Table 7.1 shows what can be done to provide experiences for males who are sensitive, gifted, gay, or dealing with ADHD to help them stay engaged in and graduate from high school.

Table 7.1: Supporting Boys Who Are Sensitive, Gay, Gifted, or ADHD to Prevent Dropout

Preschool Years (birth to age 4)	Provide gender and nongender-based examples (for example, male and female firefighters).
Boyhood (ages 5–10, kindergarten–grade 5)	Provide training to parents and teachers about boys who are sensitive, gay, gifted, or ADHD. Assess resources of students using the Personal Resource Assessments (page 101).
	School health professionals and special education personnel need to be educated about health-related behaviors, including ADHD and the side effects of various medications.
	Discourage "name calling" of students who are different.
	Teach planning to students as a way to control impulsivity.
	Teach students language to talk about feelings. Develop a Feeling-Word Thesaurus.
	Teach students to understand that all people have gifts—but they are often very different. Discuss cases where you would need one gift for one situation but another gift for another. Language arts and social studies are prime content areas for both of those discussions. "Heroes" and successful people are those who did not "fit," such as Walt Disney, Abraham Lincoln, George Washington Carver, Helen Keller, Oprah Winfrey, Steve Jobs, Bill Gates, and Albert Einstein.

continued on next page →

Adolescence (ages 11–16, grades 6–10)	Have all students assess their own resources. Ask them to complete the Future Story exercise (page 109) based on their strengths and interests.
	Discourage identification of students, especially boys, as ADHD after the age of ten: "When a previously successful boy is first 'diagnosed' with ADHD after age ten, the correct diagnosis is seldom ADHD" (Sax, 2007, p. 201).
	Educate boys and girls about how the use of derogatory words (such as *fag*) are forms of bullying.
	Have a discussion about what a "real man" is and then illustrate how different cultures view that differently. Have support groups facilitated by counselors for boys who may have issues or appear not to fit in.
	Draw attention to male writers and artists as "real men."
	Identify the characteristics of addiction (regardless of source) and the impact of addiction on lifetime success.
Early Manhood (ages 17–23, grade 11 to post–high school)	Given the accessibility and resources of the Internet, it's possible to find out a great deal about options and choices. Encourage openness to diversity.
	Have a discussion about what a "real man" is and then illustrate how different cultures view that differently. Have support groups facilitated by counselors for boys who may have issues or appear not to fit in. Provide access to adult males in diverse occupations and roles.
	Educate regarding whether it is appropriate to see medical professionals versus avoid them. Discuss how wellness and the recognition of pain are not weaknesses but rather an indicator that treatment is needed.
	Identify the characteristics of addiction (regardless of source) and its impact on lifetime success.

8 Emerging Adulthood

Researchers have begun to define young adulthood as its own developmental period, referring to it as "emerging adulthood" or "the frontier of adulthood." The daily routines that go with high school are over, and the "toddler" years of postadolescence have begun. It is becoming clear that a young man is not, at eighteen, the same person he will be at twenty-five. He doesn't look the same, feel the same, think the same, or act the same.

While legally an adult, many males at this age are as emotionally fearful as infants. According to a study by the Young Adult Development Project at the Massachusetts Institute of Technology (2008), "The years from 18 to 25 are a time of stunning accomplishments and chilling risks, as a roller coaster of internal and external changes, including brain changes, propels young adults from adolescence toward full maturity." As a number of researchers have put it, the rental car companies have it right in not allowing anyone under twenty-five to rent a car. The brain isn't fully mature at sixteen, when teens in many states are allowed to drive, or at eighteen, when we are allowed to vote, or at twenty-one, when we are allowed to drink. Age twenty-five, for many young adults, signals the dawning of a new level of maturity.

According to the Young Adult Development Project (2008):

> When teens enter young adulthood, their thinking capacities, relationship skills, and ability to regulate emotions are unlikely to be at a developmental level where they can cope easily with the demands of a diverse, global, technological, rapidly changing world.

At this age, everything that a man is supposed to be is suddenly upon him, and it is real. Yet many boys between the ages of seventeen and twenty-three have little interest in insurance, retirement plans, settling down, or beginning a career. The last part of the male brain to develop is the part that deals with long-range planning (Moir & Jessel, 1992). Instead, they're interested in cars, hanging out with friends, and dating. Most young men talk about settling down or living on their own once they get to age twenty-three or twenty-four. It is common in poverty, however, for adult males in their late twenties and early thirties to continue living at home with their mother or family. Often, this is a form of reciprocal support. When work is intermittent, or unavailable, or low paying, there is a tendency for males to live at home.

Boys from poverty who drop out of high school and don't pursue training often find themselves staying in the neighborhood, unable to find meaningful work, and lacking the support system and skills necessary to compete in the workplace. Although some get a job so they can have a car and the freedom that goes with it, the result for others is drugs, alcohol, prison, and sometimes even death.

Many boys simply lack the skills to understand the world of work. Describing a program designed to mentor teenage boys into the world of work, Canada (1998) writes:

> We find that we must train teenagers right from the beginning that a job carries with it a set of expectations that the young person might not understand or even agree with. There are the usual things that most employers expect from their employees—punctuality, good attendance, reliability. But then there are other things that we find we must instruct young people in—professional appearance, having a good attitude, respect for authority. Probably the most difficult thing our young people have to learn to cope with is how to do a good job even when you don't like doing something. It seems that many of them think they ought to like what they do for work all the time. If they don't, they often feel taken advantage of, or picked on by their supervisor, and many times they feel perfectly justified in making sure their supervisor is acutely aware of their unhappiness. (p. 111)

Canada continues:

> I have talked with many young people who have gotten fired from their jobs, and when I've questioned why they were fired they say, "They didn't like me because I'm black," or Latino, or whatever. Or they say, "They were prejudiced there. They gave me all the dirty jobs and the other

people had the easy jobs." . . . Boys often confuse their status as males with how they are treated on the job. They often feel disrespected and humiliated when a supervisor chastises them or orders them around. . . . I have found that many boys come to their first job with no real understanding of what hard work means. This is a tremendous handicap. (p. 113)

Community colleges often prepare individuals for the world of work or pursuit of a college degree. Both work and degrees require persistence and the need to deal with difficult individuals and fulfill requirements, whether you like it or not. What is often not understood is that your role does not define your self-worth. Excellence is a habit regardless of role, and self-worth may come from doing something well that adds value to a person, an organization, or a cause.

Because one feature of poverty is intermittent work or no work, there are frequently no role models of people who work, and young males do not learn the importance of persistence, task and time commitment, or of putting the work above personal feelings. If the only person insisting upon these characteristics is the boss, then he or she is seen as unfair and unreasonable, and a boy may drop out to avoid having to cope.

Post–High School Training

Young men who have dropped out of school frequently find themselves in minimum-wage jobs, where they begin to realize that they need at least a GED. Sometimes this doesn't sink in until a young man has been out of school for a couple of years.

Moreover, post–high school training of some sort is essential for today's young people. The high-tech world and the age of information have eliminated many jobs that some boys and young men could have moved into directly from high school, particularly those who want to work outside, or with their hands.

Because of maturity levels, the lack of goals, and the poor planning skills of many young males, community colleges have become viable options for many of them who return to high school or succeed in getting a GED (Weissman, Bulakowski, & Jumisko, 1998). Local community colleges enable many boys to live at home, hold a part-time job, and take those essential required courses in those first two years. Technical colleges are also viable options for some of these males, enabling them to specialize in an area of interest without the pressure of taking the English, history, and math courses that are part of a degree plan. Young adult males who seek a college degree may be ready to handle a university with a greater sense of confidence and direction after a couple of years at a community college.

Boys from poverty backgrounds who drop out of school typically lack a support system, including the relationships and role models necessary to find whatever work and training options are available. High school teachers who have formed significant relationships with boys from poverty are critical bridges for these young men. They become the external support system to help these boys make the transition from home, school, and post–high school training to the work world.

Family Expectations

For a boy from poverty who wants to return to school or get more training, one of the most difficult challenges is the conflict academic pursuits produce with family and personal relationships. Being accused of "forgetting where you came from" and being asked "Who do you think you are?" are cutting words to a young adult who often doesn't have a clear sense of direction on how to move forward. We cannot emphasize enough how crucial support systems are to these young men.

Even boys who are fortunate enough to come from families who expect them to go to college may find it very difficult to tell their parents they don't feel ready. They may give clues without coming right out and expressing their fears, as in the following hypothetical conversation:

- Parent: "What do you think you want to major in when you go to college?"

- Son: "I don't know . . . maybe some area of business." (*He is probably saying, "I don't have a clue what I want to do."*)

- Parent: "Well, you have time to make up your mind later. Where do you think you would like to go to school?"

- Son: "I don't know for sure. Charlie's going to the University of X." (*He may be saying, "I'm scared, and I would like to be somewhere with a friend."*)

- Parent: "Have you gone to the counselor and signed up for the SAT?"

- Son: "No, but I have plenty of time for that." (*He is probably saying, "I may not do well on the SAT."*)

Boys who think they must go to college to please their parents and who are afraid to be on their own are setting themselves up for failure in a way that can have enormous financial impact on a family with few financial resources.

If that same male is from poverty, this conversation would rarely occur. The conversation in poverty would go more like this:

- Parent: "After you graduate, are you going to work full time where you are working now?"

- Son: "I don't know."

- Parent: "We need the money, and if you can't get more work there, then you need to get another job."

- Son: "I know. I will."

Notice there is no future story. The conversation focuses on survival and the immediate issues. Long-range planning is nonexistent, and role identity—what you will do when you are an adult—does not occur.

Dropping Out of College

For the most part, technical school and college are rarely discussed in generational poverty. Unless a boy has a chance at a scholarship based on athletic or academic ability, college usually isn't even considered. Walpole (2003) notes that, as a result, students from poverty have always attended institutions of higher education in small numbers and are still underrepresented in four-year and more selective colleges and universities. The expectation is that you will go to work—find a job—after high school. The academic literature on the lives and experiences of poor and working-class students of all races who attend college, especially as first-generation college students, consistently demonstrates that such students know less about postsecondary education, have a more difficult transition from high school to college, and are less likely to persist and graduate than their middle-class peers (Pascarella, Pierson, Wolniak, & Terenzini, 2004; Walpole, 2003). Alexander Astin (1993) found that students' socioeconomic status (SES) is strongly correlated to virtually every measure of student satisfaction at college that he and his colleagues measured and that student SES "has its strongest effect on completion of the bachelor's degree" (p. 407).

A great deal of research points to the fact that students from poverty fail to persist in college because they feel they don't belong (Becker, Krodel, & Tucker, 2009; Cohen, 1998; Dews & Law, 1995; hooks, 2000; Jensen, 2004; Levine & Nidiffer, 1996; Nelson, Englar-Carlson, Tierney, & Hau, 2006; Roberts & Rosenwald, 2001; Stewart & Ostrove, 1993; Tokarczyk, 2004; Tokarczyk & Fay, 1993). Social class is strongly related to a sense of belonging at college, which in turn predicts social and academic adjustment, quality of experience, and academic performance (see Ostrove & Long, 2007).

A high school basketball coach in Indiana told us, with tears in his eyes, of a promising young athlete from poverty who received a four-year scholarship to Indiana University to play basketball, but left at the end of the first semester of his freshman year. The coach said that his family had called him every day, told him they missed him, and asked if he would please come home. So he did.

In educated households, parents tell stories about college—tales of the weird professors, strange roommates, and wild parties. In poverty, few people have these stories to tell, so when a young man gets to college, he enters a foreign world. Many of the people from his old neighborhood ask, "Why study when you could be earning money?" And if you are a male in poverty, there is, as we have seen, sometimes a mother and younger siblings to support and protect.

Generational poverty and the postsecondary years are often times in which individual choices determine a great deal of a boy's future. For example, having children, drug use, intermittent work history, military, technical training, life issues (death, illness, accidents), relationships, transportation, and limited resources all impact your future. In order to move out of poverty, there is a period of time in which you must give up relationships in order to pursue achievement. It is an issue of time. For students from poverty, those relationships may be family, friends, or the neighborhood. Often, however, the price is too high. In exchange for that price, you go into a world that you do not understand in which you feel your differences and your lack of resources, and you don't have money. As a matter of fact, it is a common story at universities for students from poverty who get a Pell grant to spend it on a family crisis or emergency rather than on their schooling. If you do not provide for the family, you are ostracized: "How can you be so selfish?" or "You don't love us." Or "You think you are better than we are."

Supporting Boys in the Postsecondary Years

What can be done to provide experiences for males that help them stay engaged in postsecondary education?

- Adolescents need a future story. This needs to begin very early in the educational process. Provide students with affirmative language that helps them envision what they could be. For example:

  - "You are so good at arguing, you would make a great attorney."

  - "With a smile like that, you should be a dentist."

  - "WOW! That's a great outfit. You might be a great fashion designer some day."

- "You are so good at organizing things. You might be a great parks and recreations director some day."

- Arrange visits to colleges and technical schools, particularly community colleges. Elementary students can benefit from visits to colleges and universities, especially when they see college students who mirror them racially, ethnically, and linguistically.

- Identify career choices.

- Encourage them to take a class while still in high school for "dual enrollment" to experience that environment.

- Support them in finding mentors and email buddies in career(s) in which they have an interest.

- Help them make a plan using the Future Story exercise (page 109).

- Emphasize academics whenever possible. For example, one middle school named its academic teams after Ivy League universities and adopted the mascots and school colors of those schools.

Conclusion

When a student drops out of school, everyone shares in the cost. First and foremost, the student pays a heavy price in terms of lost potential. All too often, dropouts end up as statistics in the judicial system. A large percentage of inmates in jails and prisons are high school dropouts; those inmates are funded by the taxpayers. As the workplace changes, many undereducated males find themselves unemployed and unable to secure work; unemployment also costs taxpayers. Schools lose millions of dollars in federal funding. Further, when the parents have dropped out of school, the probability that their children also will be dropouts increases, thus continuing the cycle. The cost is just too high.

Now that you have read this book, what do you do with this information? How do you create change, and how do you exert a positive impact on potential dropouts who are male and poor? First of all, remember that this is a process and not an event. It does not start in high school. If the interventions do not come until high school, it is very costly. More personnel, more interventions, more specialized classes all create more costs. The sooner the interventions, the greater the benefit and the lower the cost.

Individual Student Interventions

We recommend these steps to begin the process.

1 Use a systemic approach. If you want someone to keep from falling through the cracks, you have to identify what the cracks are. This begins when the student enrolls in school or moves into your district.

2 Take a diagnostic, not programmatic, approach. Student diagnosis must occur on a very regular basis. A "wait to fail" model should not be used; rather, a proactive approach is required from the very beginning.

3 To begin the diagnostic approach, we recommend a number of steps. When examining the following indicators, do not stereotype, but

use them as research markers whose presence increases the risk of
dropping out:

a When the student enrolls, environmental indicators that include
socioeconomic status, previous successes, the level of parental
educational attainment, ability to use age-appropriate language,
health issues (weight, hearing, and so on), gender, video-game
usage, physical activity outside of school, red-flag warnings, and
so on should be used to identify potential risk. See table 1.1,
Significant Risk Categories and Factors by School Level (page
10).

b Either through a weekend half-day session or a DVD that you
send home, let parents know the school's expectations. Don't assume they know what the expectations are, and don't wait until
there is an issue in order to articulate them. By being proactive,
future problems may be minimized.

c Use the Personal Resource Assessments (page 101) to determine
where to begin interventions and to identify a student's resources
from which you can build further resources. Interventions do
not work if the resources are not available to the student. For
example, if a student has a single parent who works two jobs, it is
not probable that the parent will be able to help the student with
schoolwork during the week. That would not be a recommended
intervention. In fact, making such demands exacerbates the issues
and creates another problem as opposed to a solution. The way
to build resources is to use existing resources and build those that
are less developed or missing.

d In generational poverty, relationships of mutual respect are
extremely important. Ask the student, "Who cares the most
about you?" and "Who do you care the most about?" If there
is no adult in that mix, that is where you begin. Find a staff
member who is willing to meet with that student one-on-one on
a regular basis. Often, the parent is not the key adult. So to have
the interventions built completely around the parent may not be
successful.

e When the parent's resources are thin or limited (the cause may
be anything—job loss, illness, divorce, homelessness, financial
issues, addiction), constantly relying upon the parent as a
problem solver only adds to the parent's feelings of inadequacy.

Ninety-nine percent of the time, the parent loves the child. Otherwise, you would have no interaction with them. Many educators assume that parents have a knowledge base of children similar to theirs. Most parents do not, so to ask the parent to be a teacher's assistant is, for many parents, to increase the likelihood of student failure. Do not confuse being loving and caring with knowledge and ability.

4 Once you have determined the presence or absence of risk indicators and have ascertained the student's access to resources, then assess physical, emotional, cognitive, and social abilities and skills.

5 From those tools, develop a plan of intervention.

This process is repeated *frequently* and revisited as a student goes through the educational system. As the physical, emotional, cognitive, or social abilities and skills change or decrease, the process must be revisited. For example, the boy fails math in a grading period. To assume that there is no problem and he will get it in the next grading period is to wait too long. When a student failure is ignored or minimized, then the problem becomes compounded, and we are literally using a "wait to fail" model.

One of the typical interventions for males in poverty is to put them in special education. In the United States, males from poverty in special education are disproportionately represented. (If you want to check this on your campus, see how many of your students in special education are male and on free or reduced lunch.) Not only does that jeopardize the student at an individual level, it also represents a system failure.

System-Level Interventions

Look for the patterns in your data. Patterns in the data tell where the system failures are. For example, if the majority of your discipline referrals are male, that indicates that the system is not "boy friendly." If a disproportional amount of special education students are from poverty, then the mainstream "program" is not responsive to under-resourced students. If you disaggregate your student performance data by gender and economic status, and there is a discrepancy between male and female performance, that would be an indicator that the current approach is not sufficient. Administrators also have to examine patterns systemwide.

Community and Neighborhood Issues

It would be remiss to think that schools alone can solve the problem of poor male dropouts. It should be noted that students who are not male and not from poverty also drop out. Ultimately, a dropout is a loss for society, for families, and of course the individual, regardless of gender or economic status.

Because schools are a part of the larger community and responsible for educating *all* students, the school becomes a key player in the economic and social well-being of the community. To abdicate that role or blame parents, students, or the community is to negate the school's mission. An analogy would be this: Every ship requires a captain and crew. The captain takes his skill and knowledge and charts a course. He does not control the weather, but he does control his crew and his ship. When the crew changes, new members must be trained.

Success

The task is not impossible, but it does require a systemic, diagnostic approach. The talent that can be developed in an individual when he is educated is phenomenal. We owe it to the greater well-being of everyone.

Appendix

Worksheet to Calculate Cost of Dropouts

What does it cost your local system when students drop out of school? Follow this process to calculate the costs. The numbers in the examples used are very conservative. In most communities, they are much higher.

First Multiplier: Cost of the Loss of Average Daily Attendance Money

1 Find the difference between the average number of students in an incoming freshman class and the average number of students in a graduating class. For example, if you have an average freshman class of 1,000, and your average senior graduating class is 600, then the difference is 400 students.

2 Multiply that number by 3. Because most students drop out during or after the ninth grade, you have three years of lost revenue.

3 Multiply the number in Step 2 by the amount the state pays for each student per year.

For example, if you have 400 fewer students graduate (on average), times 3 years, that equals 1,200 units of state payment your school does not receive. If your state pays $6,000 per student, per year, that is a loss for one class over three years of $7,200,000—or an annual loss of $2,400,000.

Second Multiplier: Cost of Repeating a Course

1 Find the average number of students who fail a required course each year and the average number of students in a class.

2 Take the average teacher salary and add $20,000 (or the amount of the average benefit package—insurance, teacher retirement, worker's compensation, and so on) in your district. Divide this number by the number of days in the teaching contract, and that gives you an average daily rate. Divide that number by the number of classes a teacher teaches per day. That becomes the cost of one period of instruction per day. Divide that cost by the average number of students in a class. That number becomes the average cost per student, per period, per day. Multiply that number by 183, and that is the annual cost of a student repeating a grade. Multiply that number by the number of students who have failed a course and had to repeat it, and you have the annual cost for all students who need to repeat a grade. (For a semester course, divide that number in half.)

For example, out of 4,000 students at a high school, 1,000 students repeat a course each semester. The average teacher salary is $40,000, plus $20,000 in benefits, which equals $60,000. The teacher is contracted for 183 days a year, which equals $328 a day. The average teacher teaches five classes a day, which comes to a daily cost of $66 per class, per day. If the teacher has, on average, 25 students in the class, that computes to $2.65 per day, per student. The cost of a student repeating that class is $2.65 × 183, which is $485. If 1,000 students have repeated a course, then the annual cost to the district is $485,000.

Third Multiplier: Personnel Time

1 Take one class and determine the number of students who dropped out. Identify the average number of hours spent on a student for one year before he or she dropped out because of discipline referrals, parent conferences, and so on. That will give you an average number of personnel hours per dropout, *before* they drop out, per year. Make certain you consider all staff members who may have been involved— for example, counselor, dean or assistant principal, principal, security, special education staff, central office staff.

2 Take the average administrative salary, and add $20,000 for benefits. Divide that number by the average number of days in the administrative contract to get a daily rate. Take that daily rate, and divide it by 8 hours in the day (a supposed workday). That is the hourly rate of administrative personnel time.

3 Multiply the average administrative hourly rate by the number of hours per dropout, and you have a personnel time cost per dropout per year.

4 Multiply that number by the number of dropouts, and you have personnel costs for dropouts for one year.

For example, in one district the average dropout received 400 hours of personnel time prior to dropping out because of discipline referrals, parent conferences, special education testing, counselor time, amount of time security spent on issues, hearings for dismissal involving the central office, and so on. The average administrative salary was $90,000, plus $20,000 for benefits, which equals $110,000. Dividing that by the 240 days in the administrative contract equals $458 per day. Dividing that by 8 hours a day (although few administrators work only eight hours a day) equals $57.25 per hour. Multiply 400 hours per dropout by the hourly rate to get $22,900 per dropout, per year, in personnel time. (Keep in mind this doesn't calculate lawyers' costs or secretarial and administrative assistant time.) So, in a school of 4,000 students, if you lose 1,000 students over 4 years, which is an average of 250 per year, you have had an additional personnel time cost of $5,725,000 per year.

Fourth Multiplier: Alternative Education Settings

Note that in most alternative settings, approximately 90 percent of the students come from poverty.

These costs vary by district. To find this cost, take the total cost for the alternative education setting (building, utilities, and personnel costs of all paid staff assigned to that building). While these facilities are designed, in part, to deal with discipline issues, the overall goal is to keep students in school. The total annual cost of these facilities is an additional cost to the district designed specifically to keep the graduation rate up while dealing with non-normative behaviors.

For example, a district has a facility that has an average of 150 students assigned to alternative school in grades 6–12. (Sometimes there are more students, sometimes there are fewer.) This alternative education setting has six teachers, one administrator, one counselor, one secretary, and one security guard. The approximate cost to the district for this facility is $960,000 annually.

Final Cost

To calculate the final cost, add the numbers together for an annual cost.

For example, the cost to the district (used in this example) per year for dropouts is $9,570,000.

Personal Resource Assessments

Use these questions both systematically and as needed to assess students' resources from kindergarten through twelfth grade.

Questions to Assess Financial Resources

Has the necessary school supplies	Yes	No
Has money for field trips	Yes	No
Has money for projects	Yes	No
Has food every evening and twice a day on weekends and holidays	Yes	No
Wears different clothing at least five days a week	Yes	No
Has more than one pair of shoes	Yes	No
Has a stable place to live (not a car or shelter; does not move every three months; is not moved from relative to relative)	Yes	No
Has books of his own	Yes	No
Has a place to study at home with good lighting	Yes	No
Has had opportunities to participate in educational activities outside of school (for example, museums, travel, camp)	Yes	No
Has access to transportation outside of school (for example, subway, bus, household vehicle)	Yes	No

From *Under-Resourced Learners: 8 Strategies to Boost Student Achievement* (pp. 3–4), by R. K. Payne, 2008, Highlands, TX: aha! Process. Copyright 2008 by aha! Process. Reprinted with permission.

Questions to Assess Language Resources

Can use formal register in the language of the dominant culture	Yes	No
Can tell a story in chronological order	Yes	No
Can get to the point in a discussion	Yes	No
Can resolve a conflict using formal register	Yes	No

continued on next page →

Can ask questions using correct syntax	Yes	No
Can write using formal organizational patterns for writing	Yes	No
Can use specific vocabulary in speech and writing	Yes	No
Can sort what is and is not important in nonfiction text	Yes	No
Can write a persuasive argument using support and logic	Yes	No

From *Under-Resourced Learners: 8 Strategies to Boost Student Achievement* (p. 5), by R. K. Payne, 2008, Highlands, TX: aha! Process. Copyright 2008 by aha! Process. Reprinted with permission.

Questions to Assess Emotional Resources

Controls impulsivity most of the time	Yes	No
Can plan for behavior and assignments	Yes	No
Controls anger	Yes	No
Has positive self-talk	Yes	No
Sees the relationship between choice and consequence	Yes	No
Can resolve a problem with words (does not hit or become verbally abusive)	Yes	No
Can stay in formal register during an argument	Yes	No
Can predict outcomes based on cause and effect	Yes	No
Can separate the behavior (criticism) from the person (contempt)	Yes	No
Has the words to name feelings	Yes	No
Can use the adult voice	Yes	No

From *Under-Resourced Learners: 8 Strategies to Boost Student Achievement* (p. 6), by R. K. Payne, 2008, Highlands, TX: aha! Process. Copyright 2008 by aha! Process. Reprinted with permission.

Questions to Assess Mental Resources

Can read at a rate that doesn't interfere with meaning	Yes	No
Can read the material required for that grade level or task	Yes	No
Can write for the task as required by school or work	Yes	No
Can add, subtract, multiply, and divide	Yes	No
Can do the math as required by the grade level or course	Yes	No
Understands money as represented on paper (checkbooks, bank statements, and so on)	Yes	No
Can operate in the paper world of school and work	Yes	No
Can use specific vocabulary related to the content or the job	Yes	No
Is test-savvy—knows how to take a test	Yes	No
Can develop questions about content or tasks on the job	Yes	No
Is organized and can find papers when they're needed (paper representation of space)	Yes	No
Can read a map	Yes	No
Has procedural self-talk	Yes	No
Can follow written directions	Yes	No
Can sequence a task or make a plan	Yes	No
Can represent an idea visually or with a story (mental models)	Yes	No
Can prioritize tasks	Yes	No
Can sort what is and is not important in a task or a text (summarization)	Yes	No
Can divide tasks into parts	Yes	No
Can get tasks or projects done on time (paper representation of time)	Yes	No
Can make to-do lists or use a planner to get things done	Yes	No

continued on next page →

Can use a calendar	Yes	No
Can tell how things are alike and different	Yes	No

From *Under-Resourced Learners: 8 Strategies to Boost Student Achievement* (pp. 7–8), by R. K. Payne, 2008, Highlands, TX: aha! Process. Copyright 2008 by aha! Process. Reprinted with permission.

Questions to Assess Spiritual Resources

Has a personal future story for himself	Yes	No
Has hope for the future (that is, believes that the future will work out in a positive way)	Yes	No
Believes in the personal ability to impact his own life (that is, does not believe he is fated)	Yes	No
Believes that there is extra support to help one with life (for example, divine guidance, a set of beliefs, prayer, meditation)	Yes	No
Has a strong personal belief system about his own positive value as a human being	Yes	No

From *Under-Resourced Learners: 8 Strategies to Boost Student Achievement* (p. 8), by R. K. Payne, 2008, Highlands, TX: aha! Process. Copyright 2008 by aha! Process. Reprinted with permission.

Questions to Assess Physical Resources

Has protein in his nutrition on a daily basis to provide memory and physical strength	Yes	No
Is healthy (usually free of illness)	Yes	No
Gets sufficient sleep (six to eight hours per night)	Yes	No
Brushes teeth on a daily basis (there is a high correlation between dental health and general health)	Yes	No
Has health insurance or access to preventive healthcare	Yes	No
Can see and hear well	Yes	No
Can move his body by himself	Yes	No
Has high levels of energy and stamina	Yes	No

Can focus the energy on a task	Yes	No
Addresses biochemical issue, if present, with either medication or a series of interventions	Yes	No
Does not use illegal drugs or alcohol	Yes	No
Engages in daily exercise	Yes	No
Has unstructured time each day to play and relax	Yes	No
Is physically fit	Yes	No
Is within the healthy height and weight range for his age	Yes	No
Is free from physical and sexual abuse	Yes	No
Has acceptable appearance (clothes, hair, and body are clean and presentable)	Yes	No

From *Under-Resourced Learners: 8 Strategies to Boost Student Achievement* (pp. 9–10), by R. K. Payne, 2008, Highlands, TX: aha! Process. Copyright 2008 by aha! Process. Reprinted with permission.

Questions to Assess Support Systems

Has parents who have at least five of the nine types of resources	Yes	No
Has parents who are supportive of school	Yes	No
Has at least two adults who care about and nurture him	Yes	No
Has at least two friends (peers) who are nurturing and not destructive	Yes	No
Belongs to a peer group (can be racial, cultural, religious, or activity-based—for example, sports, music, academics, and so on)	Yes	No
Is involved in one or more school activities (sports, music, theater, chess club, and so on)	Yes	No
Can make new friends (social capital)	Yes	No
Has at least two friends who are different from self (by race, culture, interest, academics, religion, and so on)	Yes	No
Is a mentor or a friend to whom others come for advice	Yes	No
Has at least two people who will advocate for him	Yes	No

continued on next page →

Is connected to a larger social network (bridging social capital—for example, church, 4-H, Boys & Girls Club, soccer league)	Yes	No
Can identify one group to which he belongs	Yes	No
Has at least one teacher or coach who knows him personally and will advocate for him	Yes	No
Has at least one adult who is the support system for the household and is not the student himself	Yes	No

From *Under-Resourced Learners: 8 Strategies to Boost Student Achievement* (pp. 10-11), by R. K. Payne, 2008, Highlands, TX: aha! Process. Copyright 2008 by aha! Process. Reprinted with permission.

Questions to Assess Relationships and Role Models

Has at least two friends his own age	Yes	No
Has at least one adult on the staff who knows him	Yes	No
Has at least two adults outside of school who care about him	Yes	No
Has at least one person he admires	Yes	No
Has at least one person he admires who is not a sports figure or entertainment celebrity	Yes	No
Can identify the traits he admires in a role model	Yes	No
Can identify the kind of person he does not want to be	Yes	No
Knows how to make friendships and relationships that are positive and not destructive	Yes	No
Can give and accept compliments	Yes	No
Has access to individuals who have achieved positive and nondestructive success in the dominant culture but have also retained their cultural or racial roots	Yes	No
Knows the history of his family or racial and cultural past and examples of successful individuals therefrom	Yes	No
Has an individual he can trust	Yes	No
Has role identity	Yes	No

From *Under-Resourced Learners: 8 Strategies to Boost Student Achievement* (p. 12), by R. K. Payne, 2008, Highlands, TX: aha! Process. Copyright 2008 by aha! Process. Reprinted with permission.

Questions to Assess Knowledge of Hidden Rules

Can identify and avoid the pet peeves of the person in charge (boss, teacher, for example)	Yes	No
Can identify what will actually get him into trouble at school or work, as opposed to what the rules say will get him into trouble	Yes	No
Is successful with various teachers, students, and bosses	Yes	No
Can work and learn from someone even if he does not like that person	Yes	No
Can assess a situation or person and determine which behaviors can be used and which ones cannot in order to be successful in that situation or with that person	Yes	No
Can articulate what the hidden rules are in a given situation or with a given person	Yes	No
Can differentiate between the real authority and the stated authority in a given situation	Yes	No
Knows the hidden rules of the school environment	Yes	No
Knows the hidden rules of the work environment	Yes	No
Can assess the unspoken cueing mechanisms in a given situation or with a given person and use that information to his advantage	Yes	No

From *Under-Resourced Learners: 8 Strategies to Boost Student Achievement* (p. 13), by R. K. Payne, 2008, Highlands, TX: aha! Process. Copyright 2008 by aha! Process. Reprinted with permission.

Storybook to Improve Behavior

For young children, using drawings and stories to identify appropriate behaviors is very powerful. Use this mental model with young children to help them identify appropriate behaviors.

1 Get a blank book.

2 Identify, using stick figures, the student you are working with—for example, "This is you, Robert."

3 Identify his feelings when he did the behavior—for example, "Robert is mad."

4 Identify what he actually did—for example, "Robert kicked the teacher."

5 Identify how the victim felt—for example, "Teacher is hurt. Teacher cried."

6 Identify what he could have said—for example, "I am angry because . . ."

7 Identify what his body should do—for example, "Robert's feet should be on the floor."

8 Identify how he will feel if he is doing the behavior correctly—for example, "Robert is calm."

9 Identify how the victim will feel if the student is doing the behavior correctly—for example, "Teacher is calm."

Have the student read over the pictures until he can tell the story from the pictures. When the student does the behavior, present the book and tell him to read it until he can behave appropriately. If the behavior is not in the book, someone (the principal or counselor, for example) draws it in and makes sure the student can understand it from the pictures before he leaves the office.

From *Research-Based Strategies: Narrowing the Achievement Gap for Under-Resourced Students* (p. 160), by R. K. Payne, 2009, Highlands, TX: aha! Process. Copyright 2009 by aha! Process. Reprinted with permission.

Future Story

In poverty, very few adults or children have a future story—an idea or image of what their future life could be. They typically live in the tyranny of the moment. Someone who knows he wants to attend college is not going to get stoned or miss school when there's a test. Future stories help students control impulsivity and plan. Help students develop a future story by asking them to answer the following questions.

Name:
You are ten years older than you are now. You are the star of a movie. What are you doing? Who is with you? Circle any of these that are in your future story: children, job, career, marriage or partnership, health, wealth, travel, living in a city, living in a town, living in a rural area, living in another country, vehicles, hobbies, sports, music, movies, college, technical school, military, church or religion, Internet, video games, friends, family, other.
For which of these reasons do you want to graduate from high school? To keep track of money; so I will know I am getting paid correctly; so I can go on to college or military or technical school; to get a better job; to take care of my parents or siblings; to afford my hobbies; to pay for my vehicle; to take care of my children; other.
What do you enjoy doing that you would do even if you did not get paid for it? What do you need to do so you can do that *and* get paid for doing it?
Who are the friends and adults who will help you get your future story?
Write out your future story and include how education will help you get it.
Signature:	Date:

From "Engage and Graduate Your Secondary Students: Prevent Dropouts" seminar by R. K. Payne, 2009. Copyright aha! Process. Reprinted with permission.

Graduation Plan

To help students focus on the practical and concrete aspects of what they need to do to graduate, ask them to fill out the following.

What Do I Need to Do to Graduate?

Name:	
Number of credits I need	
Tests I need to pass	
Friends who will help me get by (bonding capital)	
Friends and adults who will help me get ahead (bridging capital)	
Resources I already have that I can use	
Resources I need to develop	
New friends and adults I need to find who will help me get ahead	

From "Engage and Graduate Your Secondary Students: Prevent Dropouts" seminar by R. K. Payne, 2009. Copyright aha! Process. Reprinted with permission.

References and Resources

Abbott, D. A., Meredith, W. H., Self-Kelly, R., & Davis, M. E. (1997). The influence of a Big Brothers program on the adjustment of boys in single-parent families. *Journal of Psychology, 131*(2), 143–156.

Adelabu, D. H. (2008). Future time perspective, hope, and ethnic identity among African American adolescents. *Urban Education, 43*(3), 347–360.

Alexander, K. L., & Entwisle, D. R. (1988). Achievement in the first two years of school: Patterns and processes. *Monographs of the Society for Research in Child Development, 53*(2, Serial No. 218).

Alexander, K. L., Entwisle, D. R., & Horsey, C. S. (1997). From first grade forward: Early foundations of high school dropout. *Sociology of Education, 70*(2), 87–107.

Alexander, K. L., Entwisle, D. R., & Kabbani, N. S. (2001). The dropout process in life course perspective: Early risk factors at home and school. *Teachers College Record, 103*(5), 760–822.

Allen, G. L. (2000). Men and women, maps and minds: Cognitive bases of sex-related differences in reading and interpreting maps. In S. O. Nuallain (Ed.), *Spatial cognition: Foundations and applications* (pp. 3–18). Philadelphia: John Benjamins.

Alliance for Excellent Education. (2003a). *Factsheet: The impact of education on—crime.* Washington, DC: Author.

Alliance for Excellent Education. (2003b). *Factsheet: The impact of education on—health and well-being.* Washington, DC: Author.

Alliance for Excellent Education. (2009). *High school dropouts in America.* Accessed at www.all4ed.org/files/GraduationRates_FactSheet.pdf on February 18, 2010.

Amato, P. R. (1993). Children's adjustment to divorce: Theories, hypotheses, and empirical support. *Journal of Marriage and the Family, 55,* 23–38.

American Academy of Pediatrics. (2001). Media violence. *Pediatrics, 108*(5), 1222–1226. Accessed at http://aappolicy.aappublications.org/cgi/reprint/pediatrics;108/5/1222.pdf on March 17, 2010.

American Association of University Women Educational Foundation. (1993). *Hostile hallways: The AAUW survey on sexual harassment in America's schools.* Washington, DC: Author.

American Council for Drug Education. (n.d.). *Facts for parents: Drug education.* Accessed at www.acde.org/parent/Pregnant.htm on March 17, 2010.

American Psychiatric Association. (1994). *Diagnostic and statistical manual of mental disorders* (4th ed.). Washington, DC: Author.

Anderson, P., de Bruijn, A., Angus, K., Gordon, R., & Hastings, G. (2009). Impact of alcohol advertising and media exposure on adolescent alcohol use: A systematic review of longitudinal studies. *Alcohol and Alcoholism, 44*(3), 229–243.

Arum, R., & Beattie, I. R. (1999). High school experience and the risk of adult incarceration. *Criminology, 37*(3), 515–540.

Astin, A. W. (1993). *What matters in college? Four critical years revisited.* San Francisco: Jossey-Bass.

Baker, J. A., Bridger, R., & Evans, K. (1998). Models of underachievement among gifted preadolescents: The role of personal, family, and school factors. *Gifted Child Quarterly, 42*(1), 5–15.

Balfanz, R. (n.d.). *More information on the methodology, data, and terms used in the AP dropout factory story.* Accessed at http://web.jhu.edu/CSOS/images/AP.html on March 17, 2010.

Balfanz, R. (2007, August). *Locating and transforming the low performing high schools which produce the nation's dropouts.* Paper presented at Turning Around Low-Performing High Schools: Lessons for Federal Policy from Research and Practice, Washington, DC.

Balfanz, R., & Legters, N. (2006). Closing "dropout factories": The graduation rate crisis we know and what can be done about it. *Education Week, 25*(42), 42–43.

Bámaca, M. Y., & Umaña-Taylor, A. J. (2006). Testing a model of resistance to peer pressure among Mexican-origin adolescents. *Journal of Youth and Adolescence, 35,* 631–645.

Baron-Cohen, S. (2003). *The essential difference: The truth about the male and female brain.* New York: Basic Books.

Baron-Cohen, S., Lutchmaya, S., & Knickmeyer, R. (2004). *Prenatal testosterone in mind.* Cambridge, MA: MIT Press.

Baumeister, R. F., & Leary, M. R. (1995). The need to belong: Desire for interpersonal attachment as a fundamental human motivation. *Psychological Bulletin, 117,* 497–529.

Beals, D., De Temple, J., & Dickinson, D. (1994). Talking and listening that support early literacy development of children from low-income families. In D. Dickinson (Ed.), *Bridges to literacy: Children, families, and schools* (pp. 19–42). Cambridge, MA: Blackwell.

Beals, D., & Tabors, P. (1995). Arboretum, bureaucratic, and carbohydrates: Preschoolers' exposure to rare vocabulary at home. *First Language, 5,* 57–76.

Becker, K. A., Krodel, K. M., & Tucker, B. H. (2009). *Understanding and engaging under-resourced college students: A fresh look at the influence of economic class on teaching and learning in higher education.* Highlands, TX: aha! Process.

Belkin, A., & Bateman, G. (2003). *Don't ask, don't tell: Debating the gay ban in the military.* Boulder, CO: Lynne Rienner.

Bellinger, D., Leviton, A., Waternaux, C., Needleman, H., & Rabinowitz, C. (1987). Longitudinal analyses of prenatal and postnatal lead exposure and early cognitive development. *New England Journal of Medicine, 316,* 1037–1043.

Ben-Chaim, D., Lappan, G., & Houang, R. T. (1988). The effect of instruction on spatial visualization skills of middle school boys and girls. *American Educational Research Journal, 25*(1), 51–71.

Benenson, J. F., & Heath, A. (2006). Boys withdraw more in one-on-one interactions, whereas girls withdraw more in groups. *Developmental Psychology, 42*(2), 272–282.

Benson, C. (Ed.). (2003). *America's children: Key national indicators of well-being, 2003.* Vienna, VA: Health Resources and Services Administration Information Center.

Bergman, S. J. (2003). Men's psychological development: A relational perspective. In R. F. Levant & W. S. Pollack (Eds.), *A new psychology of men* (pp. 68–90). New York: Basic Books.

Berk, L. E. (1997). *Child development* (4th ed.). Boston: Allyn & Bacon.

Berliner, D. C. (2009). *Poverty and potential: Out-of-school factors and school success.* Accessed at http://epicpolicy.org/files/PB-Berliner-NON-SCHOOL.pdf on May 18, 2010.

Berndt, T. J., Hawkins, J. A., & Jiao, Z. (1999). Influences of friends and friendship on adjustment to junior high school. *Merrill Palmer Quarterly, 45,* 13–41.

Bethea, L. (1999). Primary prevention of child abuse. *American Family Physician.* Accessed at www.aafp.org/afp/990315ap/1577.html on March 17, 2010.

Biddulph, S. (1998). *Raising boys.* Berkeley: Celestial Arts.

Blackwell, T. (2002, May 9). Academics see sex crimes in schoolyard. *National Post.* Accessed at www.canadiancrc.com/Newspaper_Articles/Nat_Post_Academics_see _sex_crimes_in_schoolyard_09MAY02.aspx on March 17, 2010.

Bloom, S. L. (1996). *Creating sanctuary.* Oxford, England: Routledge.

Bontempo, D., & D'Augelli, A. (2002). Effects of at-school victimization and sexual orientation on lesbian, gay or bisexual youths' health risk behaviors. *Journal of Adolescent Health, 30,* 364–374.

Bradley, R. H., & Corwyn, R. F. (2002). Socioeconomic status and child development. *Annual Review of Psychology, 53,* 371–399.

Bridgeland, J. M., Dilulio, J. J., & Morison, K. B. (2006). *The silent epidemic: Perspectives of high school dropouts.* Washington, DC: Civic Enterprises, Peter D. Hart Research Associates, Bill & Melinda Gates Foundation.

British Broadcasting Company. (n.d.). *Boys growing up.* Accessed at www.bbc.co.uk/ science/humanbody/body/articles/lifecycle/teenagers/boy_s_growth.shtml on March 17, 2010.

Britz, J. D. (2006, March 23). To all the girls I've rejected. *New York Times.* Accessed at www.nytimes.com/2006/03/23/opinion/23britz.html on March 17, 2010.

Brody, L. R. (1996). Gender, emotional expression, and parent-child boundaries. In R. D. Kavanaugh, B. Zimmerberg, & S. Fein (Eds.), *Emotion: Interdisciplinary perspectives* (pp. 139–170). Mahwah, NJ: Lawrence Erlbaum Associates.

Brooks-Gunn, J., Klebanov, P. K., & Duncan, G. J. (1996). Ethnic differences in children's intelligence test scores: Role of economic deprivation, home environment, and maternal characteristics. *Child Development, 67*(2), 396–408.

Brown, B. B. (2004). Adolescents' relationships with peers. In R. Lerner & L. Steinberg (Eds.), *The handbook of adolescent psychology* (pp. 363–394). New York: John Wiley & Sons.

Brown, J. L., & Pollitt, E. (1996). Malnutrition, poverty and intellectual development. *Scientific American, 274*(2), 38–43.

Buhrmester, D. (1990). Intimacy of friendship, interpersonal competence, and adjustment during preadolescence and adolescence. *Child Development, 61,* 1101–1111.

Bullough, V. L., & Bullough, B. (1993). *Cross dressing, sex and gender.* Philadelphia: University of Pennsylvania.

Bureau of Labor Statistics. (2009). *Occupational employment, training, and earnings.* Accessed at http://data.bls.gov/oep/noeted/empoptd.jsp on March 17, 2010.

Bushman, B. J., & Huesmann, L. R. (2001). Effects of televised violence on aggression. In D. Singer & J. Singer (Eds.), *Handbook of children and the media* (pp. 223–254). Thousand Oaks, CA: SAGE.

Cagney, K. A., Glass, T. A., Skarupski, K. A., Barnes, L. L., Schwartz, B. S., & Mendes de Leon, C. F. (2009). Neighborhood-level cohesion and disorder: Measurement and validation in two older adult urban populations. *The Journals of Gerontology Series B: Psychological Sciences and Social Sciences, 64B*(3), 415–424.

Cairns, R. B., Cairns, B. D., & Neckerman, H. J. (1989). Early school dropout: Configurations and determinants. *Child Development, 60,* 1437–1452.

Campaign for Youth Justice. (2007). *Educating your legislator guide.* Accessed at www.campaign4youthjustice.org/Downloads/start/LegislativeGuide.pdf on March 17, 2010.

Campbell, K. E., & Lee, B. A. (1992). Sources of personal neighbor networks: Social, integration, need, or time? *Social Forces, 70,* 1077–1100.

Canada, G. (1998). *Reaching up for manhood: Transforming the lives of boys in America.* Boston: Beacon Press.

Capponi, P. (1997). *Dispatches from the poverty line.* Toronto: Penguin.

Cassidy, J., Parke, R. D., Butkovsky, L., & Braungart, J. M. (1992). Family-peer connections: The role of emotional expressiveness within the family and children's understanding of emotions. *Child Development, 63,* 603–618.

Cauce, A. M. (1986). Social networks and social competence: Exploring the effects of early adolescent friendships. *American Journal of Community Psychology, 14,* 607–628.

Chambers, J. G., Lam, I., Mahitivanichcha, K., Esra, P., Shambaugh, L., & Stullich, S. (2009). *State and local implementation of the No Child Left Behind Act: Volume VI—Targeting and uses of federal education funds.* Washington, DC: U.S. Department of Education Office of Planning, Evaluation and Policy Development, Policy and Program Studies Service. Accessed at www.ed.gov/rschstat/eval/disadv/nclb-targeting/nclb-targeting.pdf on March 17, 2010.

Chase-Lansdale, P. L., & Brooks-Gunn, J. (Eds.). (1997). *Escape from poverty: What makes a difference for children.* New York: Cambridge University.

Chasnoff, I. J., Anson, A., Hatcher, R., Stenson, H., Laukea, K., & Randolph, L. (1998). Prenatal exposure to cocaine and other drugs: Outcome at four to six years. *Annals of the New York Academy of Sciences, 846,* 314–328.

Chester, M. D., Offenberg, R. M., & Xu, M. D. (2001). *Urban teacher transfer: A three-year cohort study of the school district of Philadelphia faculty.* Paper presented at the annual meeting of the American Educational Research Association, Seattle, WA.

Chevannes, B. (2001). *Learning to be a man: Culture, socialization, and gender identity in five Caribbean communities.* Mona, Jamaica: University of the West Indies.

Child Welfare Information Gateway. (2008). *Long-term consequences of child abuse and neglect: Factsheet.* Accessed at www.childwelfare.gov/pubs/factsheets/long_term_consequences.cfm on March 17, 2010.

Children's Defense Fund. (n.d.). *The state of America's children 2008.* Accessed at www.childrensdefense.org/child-research-data-publications/data/state-of-americas-children-2008-report.pdf on March 17, 2010.

Clarke, J. M., Brown, J. C., & Hochstein, L. M. (1989). Institutional religion and gay/lesbian oppression. *Marriage and Family Review, 14*(3), 265–284.

Cochran, B., Stewart, A., Ginzler, J., & Cauce, A. M. (2002). Challenges faced by homeless sexual minorities: Comparison of gay, lesbian, bisexual, and transgender homeless adolescents with their heterosexual counterparts. *American Journal of Public Health, 92,* 773–793.

Cohen, D., Vandellow, J., Puente, S., & Rantilla, A. (1999). When you call me that, smile! How norms for politeness, interaction styles, and aggression work together in Southern culture. *Social Psychology Quarterly, 62*(3), 257–275.

Cohen, J. A., Mannarino, A. P., & Deblinger, E. (2006). *Treating trauma and traumatic grief in children and adolescents.* New York: Guilford Press.

Cohen, M. R. (1997). Individual and sex differences in speed of handwriting among high school students. *Perceptual and Motor Skills, 84*(3), 1428–1430.

Cohen, R. M. (1998). Class consciousness and its consequences: The impact of an elite education on mature, working-class women. *American Educational Research Journal, 35,* 353–375.

Coie, J. K., & Dodge, K. A. (1998). Aggression and antisocial behavior. In W. Damon & N. Eisenberg (Eds.), *Handbook of child psychology: Social, emotional, and personality development* (Vol. 3, 5th ed., pp. 779–862). New York: John Wiley & Sons.

Cole, B. (2007). *Spatial competence in Texas high school students.* Unpublished master's thesis, Texas State University-San Marcos. Accessed at http://ecommons.txstate.edu/honorprog/58 on March 17, 2010.

Cole, M., & Cole, S. (1993). *The development of children* (2nd ed.). New York: Scientific American Books.

Collins, J. W., Jr., David, R. J., Rankin, K. M., & Desireddi, J. R. (2009). Transgenerational effect of neighborhood poverty on low birth weight among African Americans in Cook County, Illinois. *American Journal of Epidemiology, 169*(6), 712–717.

Conway, H. W. (2006). *Collaboration for kids: Early-intervention tools for schools and communities.* Highlands, TX: aha! Process.

Corwin, M. (2001). *And still we rise: The trials and triumphs of twelve gifted inner-city high school students.* New York: Harper Perennial.

Courtney, M. (2005). *Youth aging out of foster care: Network on Transitions to Adulthood policy brief.* Philadelphia: MacArthur Foundation Research Network on Transitions to Adulthood and Public Policy.

Covey, S. R. (1989). *The 7 habits of highly effective people: Powerful lessons in personal change.* New York: Free Press.

Cox, A. (2007). *No mind left behind: Understanding and fostering executive control—The eight essential brain skills every child needs to thrive.* New York: Perigee.

Cranor, C. (1975). Toward a theory of respect for persons. *American Philosophical Quarterly, 12*(4), 309–319.

Cromie, W. J. (1998, August 6). Boys struggle to be boys. *Harvard University Gazette.* Accessed at www.news.harvard.edu/gazette/1998/08.06/BoysStruggleToB.html on March 17, 2010.

Dabney, E. (2007). *State ESEA Title I participation information for 2003–04.* Washington, DC: U.S. Department of Education Office of Planning, Evaluation and Policy Development and Office of Elementary and Secondary Education.

Damasio, A. R. (1996). *Descartes' error: Emotion, reason and the human brain.* London: Papermac.

Damasio, A. R. (2000). *The feeling of what happens.* Orlando, FL: Harcourt Brace.

D'Augelli, A., Hershberger, S., & Pilkington, N. (1998). Lesbian, gay and bisexual youth and their families: Disclosure of sexual orientation and its consequences. *American Journal of Orthopsychiatry, 68,* 361–371.

De Bellis, M., & Thomas, L. (2003). Biologic findings of post-traumatic stress disorder and child maltreatment. *Current Psychiatry Reports, 5,* 108–117.

Denham, S. A., Mitchell-Copeland, J., Strandberg, K., Auerbach, S., & Blair, K. (1997). Parental contributions to preschoolers' emotional competence: Direct and indirect effects. *Motivation and Emotion, 21,* 65–86.

Deutsch, M., Coleman, P. T., & Marcus, E. C. (Eds.). (2006). *The handbook of conflict resolution: Theory and practice.* San Francisco: Jossey-Bass.

Dews, C. L. B., & Law, C. L. (Eds.). (1995). *This fine place so far from home: Voices of academics from the working class.* Philadelphia: Temple University.

Diamond, A., & Amso, D. (2008). Contributions of neuroscience to our understanding of cognitive development. *Current Directions in Psychological Sciences, 17*(2), 136–141.

Diaz, M. A. (2008). *2008 economic downturn and federal inaction impact on crime.* Washington, DC: United States Conference of Mayors. Accessed at www.usmayors.org/mayors08actionforums/documents/CrimeReport_0808.pdf on March 19, 2010.

Dillon, R. S. (2003). Respect. In E. N. Zalta (Ed.), *The Stanford encyclopedia of philosophy.* Accessed at http://plato.stanford.edu/entries/respect/ on May 20, 2010.

Dishion, T., & Owen, L. (2002). A longitudinal analysis of friendship and substance use: Bi-directional influence from adolescence to adulthood. *Developmental Psychology, 38,* 480–489.

Donovan, J. E. (1996). Gender differences in alcohol involvement in children and adolescents: A review of the literature. *Women and Alcohol: Issues for Prevention Research* [Monograph]. Bethesda, MD: National Institute on Alcohol Abuse and Alcoholism.

Dorais, M. (2002). *Don't tell: The sexual abuse of boys.* Montreal: McGill-Queens University.

Dubow, E. F., & Ippolito, M. F. (1994). Effects of poverty and quality of the home environment on changes in the academic and behavioral adjustment of elementary school-age children. *Journal of Clinical Child Psychology, 23,* 401–412.

Duckworth, A. L., & Seligman, M. E. P. (2006). Self-discipline gives girls the edge: Gender in self-discipline, grades, and achievement test scores. *Journal of Educational Psychology, 98,* 198–208.

Dunn, J., & Brown, J. (1994). Affect expression in the family, children's understanding of emotions, and their interactions with others. *Merrill-Palmer Quarterly, 40,* 120–137.

Durham, M. (2003, March 23). Fighting fathers breed a better adjusted child, say psychologists. *Sunday Times.* Accessed at www.timesonline.co.uk/tol/news/uk/article1122404.ece on March 17, 2010.

Durston, S., Pol, H. E. H., Casey, B. J., Giedd, J. N., Buitelaar, J. K., & van Engeland, H. (2001). Anatomical MRI of the developing human brain: What have we learned? *Journal of the American Academy of Child and Adolescent Psychiatry, 40*(9), 1012–1020.

Dwyer, T., Coonan, W. E., Leitch, D. R., Hetzel, B. S., & Baghurst, P. A. (1983). An investigation of the effects of daily physical activity on the health of primary school students in South Australia. *International Journal of Epidemiology, 12,* 308–313.

Eamon, M. K. (2001). The effects of poverty on children's socioemotional development: An ecological systems analysis. *Social Work, 46*(3), 256–266.

Eaton, W., & Enns, L. (1986). Sex differences in human motor activity level. *Psychological Bulletin, 100,* 19–28.

Education Commission of the States. (2007). *The progress of education reform 2007:Dropout prevention, 8*(1). Accessed at www.ndpc-sd.org/documents/ECS/ECS-Dropout-Prevention-2007.pdf on March 17, 2010.

Egan, K., & Asher, J. (2005, June 6). *Mental illness exacts heavy toll, beginning in youth.* Accessed at www.nimh.nih.gov/science-news/2005/mental-illness-exacts-heavy-toll-beginning-in-youth.shtml on March 17, 2010.

Ekins, R., & King, D. (1996). *Blending genders: Social aspects of cross-dressing and sex-changing.* Oxford, England: Routledge.

Ekstrom, R. B., Goertz, M. E., Pollack, J. M., & Rock, D. A. (1986). Who drops out of high school and why? Findings of a national study. *Teachers College Record, 87,* 3576–3730.

Encyclopedia of Psychology. (2001). *Fine motor skills.* Accessed at http://findarticles.com/p/articles/mi_g2699/is_0004/ai_2699000469/ on March 17, 2010.

English, D. J., Widom, C. S., & Brandford, C. (2004). Another look at the effects of child abuse. *The NIJ Journal, 251,* 23–24.

Estes, S. (2005). Ask and tell: Gay veterans, identity, and oral history on a civil rights frontier. *The Oral History Review, 32*(2), 21–47.

Evans, G. W. (2004). The environment of childhood poverty. *American Psychologist, 59*(2), 77–92.

Fabes, R. A. (2003). *Emotions and the family.* Oxford, England: Routledge.

Feeding America. (2009). *One in six young children live at risk of hunger in 26 U.S. states according to new Feeding America report.* Accessed at http://feedingamerica.org/newsroom/press-release-archive/child-food-insecurity.aspx on May 20, 2010.

Feingold, A. (1993). Gender difference in mate selection preferences: A test of the parental investment model. *Psychological Bulletin, 112,* 125–139.

Fischer, C. S., & Oliker, S. J. (1983). A research note on friendship, gender, and the life cycle. *Social Forces, 62*(1), 124–133. Accessed at www.jstor.org/stable/2578351 on March 17, 2010.

Fisher, R., & Ury, W. (1983). *Getting to YES: Negotiating agreement without giving in.* New York: Penguin.

Fitchen, J. M. (1997). *Poverty in rural America: A case study.* Prospect Heights, IL: Waveland Press.

Fletcher, R. J. (2006). *Boy writers.* Portland, ME: Stenhouse.

Ford, D. Y. (1995). *A study of achievement and underachievement among gifted, potentially gifted, and regular education black students.* Storrs: University of Connecticut.

Ford, D. Y. (1996). *Reversing underachievement among gifted black students: Promising practices and programs.* New York: Teachers College Press.

Ford, D. Y., Harris, J. J., III, & Schuerger, J. M. (1993). Racial identity development among gifted black students: Counseling issues and concerns. *Journal of Counseling and Development, 71*(4), 409–417.

Fordham, S. (1988). Racelessness as a strategy in African-American students' school success: Pragmatic strategy or Pyrrhic victory? *Harvard Educational Review, 58,* 54–84.

Fordham, S., & Ogbu, J. (1986). African-American students' school success: Coping with the "burden of 'acting white.'" *Urban Review, 18,* 176–203.

Fox Chase Cancer Center. (2005). *Fox Chase Cancer Center researchers: Two compounds in plastic packaging act as environmental estrogens and can alter genes in breast tissue.* Accessed at www.fccc.edu/news/2005/Plastic-Packaging-Estrogens-04-18-05.html on May 20, 2010.

Frasier, S. D., & Rallison, M. L. (1972). Growth retardation and emotional deprivation: Relative resistance to treatment with human growth hormone. *Journal of Pediatrics, 80,* 603–609.

Freeman, J. (2002). *Media violence and its effect on aggression: Assessing the scientific evidence.* Toronto: University of Toronto.

Froehlich, J. C. (1997). Opioid peptides. *Alcohol Health and Research World, 21,* 132–135.

Gardner, H. (1993). *Frames of mind.* New York: Basic Books.

Garmezy, N. (1991). Resiliency and vulnerability to adverse developmental outcomes associated with poverty. *American Behavioral Scientist, 34*(4), 416–430.

Garmezy, N. (1993). Children in poverty: Resilience despite risk. In D. Reiss (Ed.), *Children and violence* (pp. 127–136). New York: Guilford Press.

Geary, D. C. (1996). *Children's mathematical development: Research and practical applications.* Washington, DC: American Psychological Association.

Geary, D. C., Byrd-Craven, J., Hoard, M. K., Vigil, J., & Numtee, C. (2003). Evolution and development of boys' social behavior. *Developmental Review, 23*(4), 444–470.

Ghadessy, M. (Ed.). (1988). *Registers of written English: Situational factors and linguistic features.* London: Francis Pinter.

Ghadessy, M. (Ed.). (1993). *Register analysis: Theory and practice.* London: Francis Pinter.

Gilliam, W. W. (2005). *Prekindergarteners left behind: Expulsion rates in state prekindergarten systems.* New Haven, CT: Yale University Child Study Center. Accessed at www.med .yale.edu/chldstdy/faculty/pdf/Gilliam05.pdf on March 18, 2010.

Girls get extra school help while boys get Ritalin. (2003, August 28). *USA Today.* Accessed at www.usatoday.com/news/opinion/editorials/2003–08–28-our-view_x.htm on March 22, 2010.

Gladwell, M. (2008). *Outliers: The story of success.* New York: Little, Brown.

Gladwell, M. (2009, May 11). How David beats Goliath: When underdogs break the rules. *New Yorker, 85*(13), 40–49.

Gleason, P., & Dynarski, M. (2002). Do we know whom to serve? Issues in using risk factors to identify dropouts. *Journal of Education for Students Placed at Risk, 7*(1), 25–41.

Gold, R. (2001). Confessions of a boy dancer: Running a gantlet of bullying and name-calling. *Dance Magazine, 75.* Accessed at www.thefreelibrary.com/Confessions+of +a+boy+dancer:+running+a+gantlet+of+bullying+and . . . -a080116503 on March 18, 2010.

Goldfried, M. (2001). Integrating gay, lesbian, and bisexual issues into mainstream psychology. *American Psychologist, 56,* 977–988.

Goldratt, E. M. (1999). *Theory of constraints.* Great Barrington, MA: North River Press.

Goldschmidt, P., & Wang, J. (1999). When can schools affect dropout behavior? A longitudinal multilevel analysis. *American Educational Research Journal, 36*(4), 715–738.

Goldstein, L. S. (2007). Beyond the DAP versus standards dilemma: Examining the unforgiving complexity of kindergarten teaching in the United States. *Early Childhood Research Quarterly, 22*(1), 39–54.

Goldstein, M. A., & Goldstein, M. C. (2000). *Boys into men: Staying healthy through the teen years.* Santa Barbara, CA: Greenwood Press.

Goleman, D. (2006). *Social intelligence: The new science of human relationships.* New York: Random House.

Goodwill, K. A. (2000). Religion and the spiritual needs of gay Mormon men. *Journal of Gay and Lesbian Social Services, 11*(4), 23–37.

Goodwin, L. L. (2006). *Graduating class: Disadvantaged students crossing the bridge of higher education.* Albany: State University of New York Press.

Goodwin, M. H. (1990). *He-said-she-said: Talk as social organization among black children.* Bloomington: Indiana University.

Gottman, J., Ryan, K., Swanson, C., & Swanson, K. (2003). Proximal change experiments with couples: A methodology for empirically building a science of effective interventions for changing couples' interaction. *Journal of Family Communication, 5*(3), 163–190.

Greene, J. P., & Winters, M. A. (2006). *Leaving boys behind: Public high school graduation rates—Civic report no. 48.* New York: Manhattan Institute for Policy Research. Accessed at www.manhattan-institute.org/html/cr_48.htm on March 18, 2010.

Greenspan, S. I., & Benderly, B. L. (1997). *The growth of the mind: And the endangered origins of intelligence.* New York, NY: Perseus Books.

Greenspan, S. I., & Shanker, S. G. (2006). *The first idea: How symbols, language, and intelligence evolved from our primate ancestors to modern humans.* Thousand Oaks, CA: SAGE.

Griffin, K. W., Botvin, G. J., Scheier, L. M., Diaz, T., & Miller, N. (2000). Parenting practices as predictors of substance use, delinquency, and aggression among urban minority youth: Moderating effects of family structure and gender. *Psychology of Addictive Behaviors, 14,* 174–184.

Griggs, C. (1998). *S/he: Changing sex and changing clothes.* Oxford, England: Berg.

Gross, T. (Co-executive Producer), & Miller, D. (Co-executive Producer). (2003, September 24). *Fresh air* [Radio program]. Philadelphia: WHYY-FM. Accessed at www.npr.org/templates/story/story.php?storyId=1444475 on March 19, 2010.

Gur, R. C., Turetsky, B. I., Matsui, M., Yan, M., Bilker, W., Hughett, P., et al. (1999). Sex differences in brain gray and white matter in healthy young adults: Correlations with cognitive performance. *Journal of Neuroscience, 19*(10), 4065–4072.

Gurian, M. (1998). *A fine young man: What parents, mentors, and educators can do to shape adolescent boys into exceptional men.* New York: Penguin Putnam.

Gurian, M. (1999). *The good son: Shaping the moral development of our boys and young men.* New York: Jeremy P. Tarcher.

Gurian, M. (2006). *The wonder of boys.* New York: Penguin.

Gurian, M., & Henley, P. (2001). *Boys and girls learn differently!: A guide for teachers and parents.* San Francisco: Jossey-Bass.

Gurian, M., & Stevens, K. (2005). *The minds of boys: Saving our sons from falling behind in school and life.* San Francisco: Jossey-Bass.

Gurian, M., Stevens, K., & King, K. (2008). *Strategies for teaching boys and girls.* New York: John Wiley & Sons.

Hajii. (2006). Four faces of respect. *Reclaiming Children and Youth, 15*(2), 66–70.

Halpern, D. F. (2000). *Sex differences in cognitive abilities* (3rd ed.). Mahwah, NJ: Lawrence Erlbaum Associates.

Hammond, C., Linton, D., Smink, J., & Drew, S. (2007). *Dropout risk factors and exemplary programs.* Clemson, SC: National Dropout Prevention Center, Communities in Schools.

Hantover, J. P. (1978). The Boy Scouts and the validation of masculinity. *Journal of Social Issues, 34,* 184–195.

Harding, D. J. (2009). Violence, older peers, and the socialization of adolescent boys in disadvantaged neighborhoods. *American Sociological Review, 74*(3), 445–464.

Harlow, C. W. (2003). *Education and correctional populations: Bureau of Justice Statistics special report.* Washington, DC: U.S. Department of Justice.

Harrison, S. D. (2002, August). *Devaluing femininity: Its role in determining musical participation by boys.* Paper presented at the International Society for Music Education Conference, Bergen, Norway.

Hart, A. D. (2007). *Thrilled to death: How the endless pursuit of pleasure is leaving us numb.* Nashville, TN: Thomas Nelson.

Hart, B., & Risley, T. R. (1992). American parenting of language-learning children: Persisting differences in family-child interactions observed in natural home environments. *Developmental Psychology, 28*(6), 1096–1105.

Hart, B., & Risley, T. R. (1995). *Meaningful differences in the everyday experience of young American children.* Baltimore: Paul H. Brookes.

Hart, B., & Risley, T. R. (1999). *The social world of children: Learning to talk.* Baltimore: Paul H. Brookes.

Hart, B., & Risley, T. R. (2003). The early catastrophe: The 30 million word gap. *American Educator, 27*(1), 4–9.

Hart, S. G., & Staveland, L. E. (1988). Development of NASA-TLX (task load index): Results of empirical and theoretical research. In P. A. Hancock & N. Meshkati (Eds.), *Human mental workload* (pp. 139–183). New York: Elsevier Science Publishing Company. Accessed at http://humansystems.arc.nasa.gov/groups/TLX/downloads/NASA -TLXChapter.pdf on March 18, 2010.

Hatch, J. A. (2004). *Teaching in the new kindergarten.* Clifton, NY: Thomson Delmar Learning.

Hausman, B. L. (1995). *Changing sex: Transsexualism, technology, and the idea of gender.* Durham, NC: Duke University.

Henderson, N., & Milstein, M. M. (2003). *Resiliency in schools: Making it happen for students and educators.* Thousand Oaks, CA: Corwin Press.

Herman-Jeglinska, A., Grabowska, A., & Dulko, S. (2002). Masculinity, femininity and transsexualism. *Archives of Sexual Behavior, 31*(6), 527–534.

Hingson, R., & Kenkel, D. (2004). Social, health, and economic consequences of underage drinking. In R. J. Bonnie & M. E. O'Connell (Eds.), *Reducing underage drinking: A collective responsibility* (pp. 351–382). Washington, DC: National Academies Press. Accessed at www.nap.edu/books/0309089352/html on March 18, 2010.

Hirsch, B. J., & DuBois, D. L. (1992). The relation of peer social support and psychological symptomatology during the transition to junior high school: A two-year longitudinal analysis. *American Journal of Community Psychology, 20,* 333–347.

Hobbs, R. (2000). *Media literacy* [Curriculum]. New York, NY: Newsweek Education. Accessed at http://education.stateuniversity.com/pages/2212/Media-Influence-on -Children.html on May 19, 2010

Hofstede, G. (2002). *Culture's consequences: International differences in work related values* (2nd ed.). Thousand Oaks, CA: SAGE.

Honora, D. T. (2002). The relationship of gender and achievement to future outlook among African American adolescents. *Adolescence, 37*(146), 300–316.

hooks, b. (2000). *Where we stand: Class matters.* New York: Routledge.

Hormone-mimics in plastic water bottles act as functional estrogens. (2009, March 27). *ScienceDaily.* Accessed at www.sciencedaily.com/releases/2009/03/090326100714.htm on March 18, 2010.

Howard, P. J. (2006). *The owner's manual for the brain: Everyday applications from mind-brain research* (3rd ed.). Austin, TX: Bard Press.

Howell, E. F. (2002). Back to the "states": Victim and abuser states in borderline personality disorder. *Psychoanalytic Dialogues: The International Journal of Relational Perspective, 12*(6), 921–957.

Human Rights Watch. (2001). *Hatred in the hallways: Violence and discrimination against gay, lesbian, bisexual and transgender students in the U.S.* New York: Author.

Hunter, A. G., & Davis, J. E. (1992). Constructing gender: An exploration of Afro-American men's conceptualization of manhood. *Gender and Society, 6*(3), 464–479.

Hunter, A. G., & Davis, J. E. (1994). *Hidden voices of black men: The meaning, structure, and complexity of manhood.* Thousand Oaks, CA: SAGE.

Hyde, J. S. (2005). The gender similarities hypothesis. *American Psychologist, 60*(6), 581–592.

Hyde, J., & Linn, M. (1988). Gender differences in verbal ability: A meta-analysis. *Psychological Bulletin, 104*(1), 53–69.

Iannelli, V. (2010). *Child abuse statistics.* Accessed at http://pediatrics.about.com/od/childabuse/a/05_abuse_stats.htm on May 20, 2010.

Iceland, J. (2003). *Poverty in America.* Los Angeles: University of California.

Jackson, D. (1990). *Unmasking masculinity.* London: Unwin Hyman.

Jackson, P. S. (1995). *Bright star, black sky: Origins and manifestations of the depressed state in the lived experience of the gifted adolescent—A phenomenological study.* Unpublished master's thesis, Vermont College, Norwich University.

Jackson, P. S., & Peterson, J. (2003). Depressive disorder in highly gifted adolescents. *Journal of Secondary Gifted Education, 14*(3), 175–186.

Janosz, M., Le Blanc, M., Boulerice, B., & Tremblay, R. E. (1997). Disentangling the weight of school dropout predictors: A test on two longitudinal samples. *Journal of Youth and Adolescence, 26,* 733–762.

Jarrell, A. (2000, April 2). The face of teenage sex grows younger. *New York Times.* Accessed at www.nytimes.com/2000/04/02/style/the-face-of-teenage-sex-grows-younger.html?scp=1&sq=the%20face%20of%20teenage%20sex%20grows%20younger&st=cse on July 15, 2010.

Jensen, B. (2004). Across the great divide: Crossing classes and clashing cultures. In M. Zweig (Ed.), *What's class got to do with it? American society in the twenty-first century* (pp. 168–183). Ithaca, NY: Cornell University.

Jimerson, S., Egeland, B., Sroufe, L. A., & Carlson, B. (2000). A prospective longitudinal study of high school dropouts examining multiple predictors across development. *Journal of School Psychology, 38*(6), 525–549.

Johnson, C. C., & Johnson, K. A. (2000). High-risk behavior among gay adolescents: Implications for treatment and support. *Adolescence, 35*(140), 619–637.

Johnson, J. G., Cohen, P., Smailes, E. M., Kasen, S., & Brook, J. S. (2002). Television viewing and aggressive behavior during adolescence and adulthood. *Science, 295,* 2468–2471.

Johnson, R., Rew, L., & Sternglanz, R. W. (2006). The relationship between childhood sexual abuse and sexual health practices of homeless adolescents. *Adolescence, 41*(162), 221–234.

Jones, H. M. F. (2002). Respecting respect: Exploring a great deal. *Educational Studies, 28*(4), 341–352.

Jones, J. L. (1999). *The psychotherapist's guide to human memory.* New York: Basic Books.

Jordan, B. (1996). *A theory of poverty and social exclusion.* Cambridge, MA: Blackwell.

Jordan, E. (1995). Fighting boys and fantasy play: The construction of masculinity in the early years of school. *Gender and Education, 7*(1), 69–86. Accessed at www.informaworld.com/smpp/title~db=all~content=t713422725~tab=issueslist ~branches=7—v7 on March 18, 2010.

Jordan, W. J., Lara, J., & McPartland, J. M. (1994). *Exploring the complexity of early dropout causal structures: Report no. 48.* Baltimore: Center for Research on Effective Schooling for Disadvantaged Students, Johns Hopkins University.

Jordan, W. J., McPartland, J. M., & Lara, J. (1999). Rethinking the causes of high school dropout. *Prevention Researcher, 6*(3), 1–4.

Juszkiewicz, J. (2000). *Youth crime/adult time: Is justice served?* Washington, DC: Pretrial Services.

Kantor, M. (1998). *Homophobia: Description, development, and dynamic of gay bashing.* Westport, CT: Praeger.

Kaufman, P., Bradbury, D., & Owings, J. (1992). *Characteristics of at-risk students in the NELS:88.* Washington, DC: National Center for Education Statistics, Office of Educational Research and Improvement, U.S. Department of Education.

Kelley, B. T., Thornberry, T. P., & Smith, C. A. (1997). *In the wake of childhood maltreatment.* Washington, DC: National Institute of Justice. Accessed at www.ncjrs.gov/pdffiles1/165257.pdf on March 18, 2010.

Kerr, B., & Cohn, S. (2001). *Smart boys: Talent, manhood, and the search for meaning.* Scottsdale, AZ: Great Potential Press.

Kiesner, J., Cadinu, M., Poulin, F., & Bucci, M. (2002). Group identification in early adolescence: Its relation with peer adjustment and its moderator effect on peer influence. *Child Development, 73,* 196–208.

Kimmel, M. S. (2000). *The gendered society.* New York: Oxford University.

Kimmel, M. S. (2005). *The history of men.* Albany: State University of New York Press.

Kimmel, M. S., & Aronson, A. (2003). *Men and masculinities.* Oxford, England: ABC-Clio.

Kimmel, M. S., & Mahler, M. (2003). Adolescent masculinity, homophobia, and violence: Random school shootings, 1982–2001. *American Behavioral Scientist, 46*(10), 1439–1458.

Kindlon, D., & Thompson, M. (2000). *Raising Cain: Protecting the emotional life of boys.* New York: Ballantine Books.

Kiselica, M., Englar-Carlson, M., & Horne, A. M. (2007). *Counseling troubled boys.* New York: Routledge.

Kishiyama, M. M., Boyce, W. T., Jimenez, A. M., Perry, L. M., & Knight, R. T. (2009). Socioeconomic disparities affect prefrontal function in children. *Journal of Cognitive Neuroscience, 21*(6), 1106–1115.

Kitts, R. L. (2005). Gay adolescents and suicide: Understanding the association. *Adolescence, 40*(159), 621–628.

Klein, K. (n.d.). *Why boys need rough-and-tumble play.* Accessed at www.babyzone.com/toddler_preschooler_fun/play/article/boys-need-rough-tumble-play on March 18, 2010.

Kolb, B., & Whishaw, I. Q. (2008). *Fundamentals of human neuropsychology*. New York: Macmillan.

Kübler-Ross, E. (1969). *On death and dying*. New York: Simon & Schuster.

Kumpulainen, K., & Roine, S. (2002). Depressive symptoms at the age of 12 years and future heavy alcohol use. *Addictive Behaviors, 27*(3), 425–436.

Laird, J., Cataldi, E. F., KewalRamani, A., & Chapman, C. (2008). *Dropout and completion rates in the United States: 2006* (NCES 2008–053). Washington, DC: National Center for Education Statistics, Institute of Education Sciences, U.S. Department of Education. Accessed at http://nces.ed.gov/pubsearch/pubsinfo.asp?pubid=2008053 on March 18, 2010.

Lareau, A. (2003). *Unequal childhoods: Class, race and family life*. Berkeley: University of California.

Lawrence, A. A. (2003). Normal: Transsexual CEOs, cross-dressing cops, and hermaphrodites with attitude. *Archives of Sexual Behavior, 32,* 387–388.

Lecanuet, J. P. (1995). *Fetal development: A psychobiological perspective*. Hillsdale, NJ: Lawrence Erlbaum Associates.

LeDoux, J. (1996). *The emotional brain*. New York: Simon & Schuster.

Lee, R. (2005, April 15). "Boy-code" a factor in fatal school shootings? *Washington Blade*. Accessed at www.washblade.com/2005/4–15/news/national/boycode.cfm on January 3, 2006.

Lehr, C. A., Johnson, D. R., Bremer, C. D., Cosio, S., & Thompson, M. (2004). *Essential tools: Increasing rates of school completion—Moving from policy and research to practice*. Minneapolis, MN: National Center on Secondary Education and Transition.

Levant, R. F., & Pollack, W. S. (Eds.). (2003). *A new psychology of men*. New York: Basic Books.

LeVay, S., & Hamer, D. (1994). Evidence for a biological influence in male homosexuality. *Scientific American, 270,* 44–49.

Levine, A., & Nidiffer, J. (1996). *Beating the odds: How the poor get to college*. San Francisco: Jossey-Bass.

Lewis, A. C. (1996). Breaking the cycle of poverty. *Phi Delta Kappan, 78*(3), 186–187.

Liming, D., & Wolf, M. (2008). Job outlook by education, 2006–16. *Occupational Outlook Quarterly*. Accessed at www.bls.gov/opub/ooq/2008/fall/art01.pdf on March 17, 2010.

Lindahl, L. B., & Heimann, M. (1997). Social proximity in early mother-infant interactions: Implications for gender differences? *Early Development and Parenting, 6,* 83–88.

Lindsey, E. W., Mize, J., & Pettit, G. S. (1997). Differential play patterns of mothers and fathers of sons and daughters: Implications for children's gender role development. *Sex Roles, 37,* 643–661.

Lindstrom, R. R., & Van Sant, S. (1986). Special issues in working with gifted minority adolescents. *Journal of Counseling and Development, 64*(9), 583–586.

Linn, M. C., & Peterson, A. C. (1985). Emergence and characterization of sex differences in spatial ability: A meta-analysis. *Child Development, 56,* 1479–1498.

Linver, M., Martin, A., & Brooks-Gunn, J. (2004). Measuring infants' home environment: The IT-HOME for infants between birth and 12 months in four national data sets. *Parenting, 4*(2), 115–137.

Lipkin, A. (1999). *Understanding homosexuality, changing schools: A text for teachers, counselors, and administrators.* Boulder, CO: Westview Press.

Llinas, R. R., & Churchland, P. S. (1996). *The mind-brain continuum.* Cambridge, MA: MIT Press.

Lupien, S. J., King, S., Meaney, M. J., & McEwen, B. S. (2000). Child's stress hormone levels correlate with mother's socioeconomic status and depressive state. *Biological Psychiatry, 48,* 976–980.

Maccoby, E. E. (1998). *The two sexes: Growing up apart, coming together.* Cambridge, MA: Harvard University.

MacGillis, A. (2009, July 27). Poor neighborhoods key to future income, study finds. *Washington Post.* Accessed at www.washingtonpost.com/wp-dyn/content/article/2009/07/26/AR2009072602347.html on August 30, 2009.

MacLeod, J. (1995). *Ain't no makin' it: Aspirations and attainment in a low-income neighborhood.* Boulder, CO: Westview Press.

Mahoney, P. (1985). *Schools for the boys?* London: Hutchinson.

Marshall, J. (2003). Children and poverty: Some questions answered. *Childhood Poverty Research and Policy Centre Briefing 1.* Accessed at www.childhoodpoverty.org/index.php?action=publicationdetails&id=46 on March 18, 2010.

Marusza, J. (2004). Skill school boys: Masculine identity formation among white boys in an urban high school vocational autoshop program. *Urban Review, 29*(3), 175–187.

Marzano, R. J. (2004). *Building background knowledge for academic achievement: Research on what works in schools.* Alexandria, VA: Association for Supervision and Curriculum Development.

Marzano, R. J., & Pickering, D. J. (2005). *Building academic vocabulary: Teacher's manual.* Alexandria, VA: Association for Supervision and Curriculum Development.

Masters, M. S., & Sanders, B. (1993). Is the gender difference in mental rotation disappearing? *Behavior Genetics, 23,* 337–341.

Masters, W. H., & Johnson, V. E. (1979). *Homosexuality in perspective.* New York: Little, Brown.

Matthews, F. (1996). *The invisible boy: Revisioning the victimization of male children and teens.* Ottawa, Canada: National Clearinghouse on Family Violence.

Mau, W. C. (1995). Educational planning and academic achievement of middle school students: A racial and cultural comparison. *Journal of Counseling and Development, 73,* 518–534.

Mau, W. C., & Bikos, L. M. (2000). Educational and vocational aspirations of minority and female students: A longitudinal study. *Journal of Counseling and Development, 78,* 186–194.

Mau, W. C., Hitchcock, R., & Calvert, C. (1998). High school students' career plans: The influence of others' expectations. *Professional School Counseling, 2,* 161–166.

Mau, W., & Lynn, R. (2000). Gender differences in homework and test scores in mathematics, reading and science at tenth and twelfth grade. *Psychology, Evolution, and Gender, 2,* 119–125.

Mayer, S. E. (1997). *What money can't buy.* Cambridge, MA: Harvard University.

McEwan, B. S., & Seeman, T. (1999). Protective and damaging effects of mediators of stress: Elaborating and testing the concepts of allostasis and allostatic load. *Annals of the New York Academy of Sciences, 896,* 30–47.

McGee, J. P., & DeBernardo, C. R. (1999). *The classroom avenger: School shooting case studies.* Baltimore: Sheppard and Enoch Pratt Health System.

McLanahan, S. (1985). Family structure and the reproduction of poverty. *American Journal of Sociology, 90*(4), 873–901.

Mechling, J. (2001). *On my honor: Boy Scouts and the making of American youth.* Chicago: University of Chicago.

Medical News. (2004, August 5). *More young men turning to Viagra.* Accessed at www .news-medical.net/news/2004/08/05/3808.aspx on March 19, 2010.

Medical News Today. (2004, September 14). *Risk of ADHD greater in boys.* Accessed at www.medicalnewstoday.com/articles/13411.php on March 19, 2010.

Mehta, P. H., & Josephs, R. A. (2006). Testosterone change after losing predicts the decision to compete again. *Hormones and Behavior, 50*(5), 684–692.

Mersch, J. (2009). *Child abuse.* Accessed at www.medicinenet.com/child_abuse/article.htm on March 19, 2010.

Meyer, E. J. (2009). *Gender, bullying, and harassment: Strategies to end sexism and homophobia in schools.* New York: Teachers College Press.

Moir, A., & Jessel, D. (1992). *Brain sex: The real difference between men and women.* Peaslake, England: Delta.

Monroe, S. M. (2008). Modern approaches to conceptualizing and measuring human life stress. *Annual Review of Clinical Psychology, 4,* 33–52.

Montaño-Harmon, M. R. (1991). Discourse features of written Mexican Spanish: Current research in contrastive rhetoric and its implications. *Hispania, 74*(2), 417–425.

Moore, D., & Davenport, S. (1990). School choice: The new and improved sorting machine. In W. L. Boyd & H. J. Walberg (Eds.), *Choice in education: Potentials and problems* (pp. 187–222). Berkeley: McCutchan.

Moore, G. (1990). Structural determinants of men's and women's personal networks. *American Sociological Review, 55*(5), 726–735. Accessed at www.jstor.org/stable/2095868 on March 19, 2010.

Moore, J. L., III, Ford, D. Y., & Milner, H. R. (2005). Underachievement among gifted students of color: Implications for educators. *Theory Into Practice.* Accessed at http://findarticles.com/p/articles/mi_m0NQM/is_2_44/ai_n13783933/ pg_9/?tag=content;co11 on March 19, 2010.

Morgan, S., & O'Leary, L. (2009). *City crime rankings 2008–2009: Crime in metropolitan America* (15th ed.). Washington, DC: Congressional Quarterly.

Morose, R. (2006). *The mind of consciousness.* Ocean Shores, Australia: Ocean View.

Moynihan, D. P. (1986). *Family and nation.* Orlando, FL: Harcourt Brace Jovanovich.

Mozes, A. (2008, February 21). Poverty drains nutrition from family diet. *Washington Post.* Accessed at www.washingtonpost.com/wp-dyn/content/article/2008/02/21/AR2008022101091.html on March 19, 2010.

Mullen, P. E., Martin, J. L., Anderson, J. C., Romans, S. E., & Herbison, G. P. (1996). The long-term impact of physical, emotional, and sexual abuse of children: A community study. *Child Abuse and Neglect, 20,* 7–21.

Myers, D. L. (2004). *Boys among men: Trying and sentencing juveniles as adults.* Westport, CT: Praeger.

Nabhan, G. P., & Trimble, S. (1994). *The geography of childhood.* Boston: Beacon Press.

Najman, J. M., Aird, R., Bor, W., O'Callaghan, M., Williams, G. M., & Shuttlewood, G. J. (2004). The generational transmission of socioeconomic inequalities in child cognitive development and emotional health. *Social Science and Medicine, 58*(6), 1147–1158.

National Association for Sport and Physical Education. (2000). *Public attitudes toward physical education: Are schools providing what the public wants?* Reston, VA: Author.

National Center on Addiction and Substance Abuse. (2003). *Formative years: Pathways to substance abuse among girls and young women ages 8–22.* New York: Columbia University.

National Center on Addiction and Substance Abuse. (2008). *National survey of American attitudes on substance abuse XIII: Teens and parents.* New York: Author.

National Center on Addiction and Substance Abuse. (2009). *The importance of family dinners.* Accessed at www.casacolumbia.org/articlefiles/380-Importance%20of%20Family%20Dinners%20IV.pdf on May 20, 2010

National Center for Health Statistics. (2007). *Health, United States, 2007 with chartbook on trends in the health of Americans.* Hyattsville, MD: Author.

National Dropout Prevention Center for Students with Disabilities. (2008). *An analysis of state performance plan data for indicator 2 (dropout).* Clemson, SC: Author.

National Institute on Drug Abuse. (2005). *Monitoring the future.* Bethesda, MD: Author.

Nelson, J. (1997). Gay, lesbian, and bisexual adolescents: Providing esteem-enhancing care to a battered population. *Nurse Practitioner, 22,* 94–109.

Nelson, M. L., Englar-Carlson, M., Tierney, S. C., & Hau, J. M. (2006). Class jumping into academia: Multiple identities for counseling academics. *Journal of Counseling Psychology, 53,* 1–14.

Neu, T. W., & Weinfeld, R. (2007). *Helping boys succeed in school.* Waco, TX: Prufrock Press.

Newman, B. M., Lohman, B. J., & Newman, P. R. (2007). Peer group membership and a sense of belonging: Their relationship to adolescent behavior problems. *Adolescence, 42*(166), 241–263.

Newman, B. S., & Muzzonigro, P. G. (1993). The effects of traditional family values on the coming out process of gay male adolescents. *Adolescence, 28*(109), 213–226.

Newman, M., Woodcock, A., & Dunham, P. (2006). "Playtime in the borderlands": Children's representations of school, gender and bullying through photographs and interviews. *Children's Geographies, 4*(3), 289–302.

Nurmi, J. E. (1991). How do adolescents see their future? A review of the development of future orientation and planning. *Developmental Review, 11,* 1–59.

Nurmi, J. E. (2004). Socialization and self development: Channeling, selection, adjustment, and reflection. In R. Lerner and L. Steinberg (Eds.), *Handbook of adolescent psychology* (pp. 85–124). New York: John Wiley & Sons.

Office of Applied Studies. (2007). *Results from the 2006 national survey on drug use and health: National findings* (DHHS Publication No. SMA 07–4293, NSDUH Series H-32). Rockville, MD: Substance Abuse and Mental Health Services Administration. Accessed at http://oas.samhsa.gov/p0000016.htm on March 19, 2010.

Office of Applied Studies. (2008). *The relationship between mental health and substance abuse among adolescents: Findings* (OAS Analytic Series #9, DHHS Publication No. SMA 99–3286). Rockville, MD: Substance Abuse and Mental Health Services. Accessed at www.oas.samhsa.gov/nhsda/a-9/toc.htm on March 19, 2010.

Office of Juvenile Justice and Delinquency Prevention. (2006). *Upper age of jurisdiction.* Washington, DC: U.S. Department of Justice.

Ogbu, J. U. (2003). *Black American students in an affluent suburb: A study of academic disengagement.* Mahwah, NJ: Lawrence Erlbaum Associates.

Olweus, D. (1993). *Bullying at school: What we know and what we can do.* Cambridge, MA: Blackwell.

Online Education. (2009) *Videogame statistics.* Accessed at www.onlineeducation.net/videogame on May 20, 2010.

Osofsky, J. D. (1998). *Children in a violent society.* New York: Guilford Press.

Ostrove, J. M., & Long, S. M. (2007). Social class and belonging: Implications for college adjustment. *The Review of Higher Education, 30*(4), 363–389.

Oyserman, D., Brickman, D., Bybee, D., & Celious, A. (2006). Fitting in matters: Markers of in-group belonging and academic outcomes. *Psychological Science, 17*(10), 854–861.

Palinscar, A. S., & Brown, A. L. (1984). Reciprocal teaching of comprehension-fostering and comprehension-monitoring activities. *Cognition and Instruction, 1*(2), 117–175.

Pascarella, E. T., Pierson, C. T., Wolniak, G. C., & Terenzini, P. T. (2004). First generation college students: Additional evidence on college experiences and outcomes. *Journal of Higher Education, 75,* 249–284.

Pascoe, C. J. (2007). *Dude, you're a fag: Masculinity and sexuality in high school.* Berkeley: University of California.

Patlak, M., & Joy, J. E. (2002). *Is soccer bad for children's heads? Summary of the IOM workshop on neuropsychological consequences of head impact in youth soccer.* Washington, DC: National Academies of Science, Institute of Medicine. Accessed at www.nap.edu/openbook .php?isbn=0309083443 on March 19, 2010.

Paymar, M. (2000). *Violent no more.* Alameda, CA: Hunter House.

Payne, R. K. (2005). *A framework for understanding poverty* (4th ed.). Highlands, TX: aha! Process.

PBS Parents. (n.d.). *Understanding and raising boys: Active or aggressive boys?* Accessed at www .pbs.org/parents/raisingboys/aggression.html on March 15, 2010.

PE4life. (2007). *Results.* Accessed at www.pe4life.org/about-us/results/ on May 20, 2010.

Pearce, M. J., Jones, S. M., Schwab-Stone, M. E., & Ruchkin, V. (2003). The protective effects of religiousness and parent involvement on the development of conduct problems among youth exposed to violence. *Child Development, 74*(6), 1682–1696.

Pease, B., & Pease, A. (2000). *Why men don't listen and women can't read maps: How we're different and what to do about it.* New York: Broadway Books.

Pendleton, A., & Stullich, S. (2008). *National assessment of Title I final report* [Digital slide presentation]. Accessed at http://ies.ed.gov/ncee/pubs/20084012/slides.asp?ppt=NATI on March 19, 2010.

Pereira, M. E., & Fairbanks, L. A. (2002). *Juvenile primates: Life history, development, and behavior.* New York: Oxford University.

Phillips, L., & Garrett, E. M. (in press). *Why don't they just get a job? One couple's mission to end poverty in their community.* Highlands, TX: aha! Process.

Pierangelo, R., & Giuliani, G. A. (2008). *Classroom management for students with emotional and behavioral disorders.* Thousand Oaks, CA: Corwin Press.

Pierce, C. (1994). Importance of classroom climate for at-risk learners. *Journal of Educational Research, 88*(1), 37–42.

Pikulski, J. J., & Templeton, S. (2004). *Teaching and developing vocabulary: Key to long-term reading success.* Geneva, IL: Houghton Mifflin. Accessed at www.eduplace.com/state/author/pik_temp.pdf on March 19, 2010.

Pilkington, N. W., & D'Augelli, A. R. (1995). Victimization of lesbian, gay and bisexual youth in community settings. *Journal of Community Psychology, 23*(1), 33–56.

Pitcher, E. G., & Schultz, L. H. (1983). *Boys and girls at play: The development of sex roles.* South Hadley, MA: Bergin & Garvey.

Pleck, J. H. (1981). *The myth of masculinity.* Cambridge, MA: MIT Press.

Poest, C. A., Williams, J. R., Witt, D., & Atwood, M. E. (1989). Physical activity patterns of preschool children. *Early Childhood Research Quarterly, 4,* 367–376.

Polce-Lynch, M., Myers, B. J., Kliewer, W., & Kilmartin, C. (2001). Adolescent self-esteem and gender: Exploring relations to sexual harassment, body image, media influence, and emotional expression. *Journal of Youth and Adolescence, 30,* 225–244.

Pollack, W. (1998). *Real boys: Rescuing our sons from myths of boyhood.* New York: Henry Holt.

Pollack, W. (2000). *Real boys' voices.* New York: Random House.

Postman, N. (1985). *Amusing ourselves to death.* New York: Penguin.

Putnam, R. D. (2000). *Bowling alone: The collapse and revival of American community.* New York: Simon & Schuster.

Ratey, J. J., & Hagerman, E. (2007). *Spark: The revolutionary new science of exercise and the brain.* New York: Little, Brown.

Rath, T. (2007). *Strengthsfinder 2.0.* Washington, DC: Gallup Press.

Reisberg, D., & Hertel, P. (2004). *Memory and emotion.* New York: Oxford University.

Renchler, R. (1993). *Poverty and learning.* Accessed at http://eric.ed.gov/ERICDocs/data/ericdocs2sql/content_storage_01/0000019b/80/29/a6/8a.pdf on May 20, 2010.

Reynolds, J. R., & Pemberton, J. (2001). Rising college expectations among youth in the United States: A comparison of the 1979 and 1997 NLSY. *Journal of Human Resources, 36,* 703–726.

Rhea, D. J. (2009, July 2). Fixing the problems of high school P.E. *Education Week.* Accessed at www.edweek.org/ew/articles/2009/07/02/36rhea.h28.html on May 20, 2010.

Ricciuti, H. H. (1993). Nutrition and mental development. *Current Directions in Psychological Science, 2,* 43–46.

Rivers, I., Duncan, N., & Besag, V. E. (2007). *Bullying: A handbook for educators and parents.* Westport, CT: Praeger.

Rizzo, R., & Parks, L. (2007). *The culture of generational poverty: Providing meaningful help to the impoverished.* Washington, DC: SpeedyCEUS, National Association of Social Workers. Accessed at www.ceus-nursing.com/ceus-courses/material_detail.php?id=120 on March 19, 2010.

Roberts, J. S., & Rosenwald, G. C. (2001). Ever upward and no turning back: Social mobility and identity formation among first-generation college students. In D. P. McAdams, R. Josselson, & A. Lieblich (Eds.), *Turns in the road: Narrative studies of lives in transition* (pp. 91–119). Washington, DC: American Psychological Association.

Rogers, L., & Hallam, S. (2006). Gender differences in approaches to studying among high-achieving pupils. *Educational Studies, 32,* 59–71.

Rorabaugh, W. J. (1988). *The craft apprentice.* New York: Oxford University.

Rouse, C. E. (2005, October). *Labor market consequences of an inadequate education.* Paper presented at the Symposium on the Social Costs of Inadequate Education, Teachers College, Columbia University, New York, NY.

Rumberger, R. W. (2001, January). *Why students drop out of school and what can be done.* Paper presented at Dropouts in America: How Severe Is the Problem? What Do We Know About Intervention and Prevention? Cambridge, MA.

Russell, S., Franz, B., & Driscoll, A. (2001). Same-sex romantic attraction and experiences of violence in adolescence. *American Journal of Public Health, 91,* 903–906.

Saarni, C. (1999). *The development of emotional competence.* New York: Guilford Press.

Salazar, M. (2009, August 4). State: Almost half of class of 2008 didn't graduate. *Albuquerque Journal.* Accessed at www.abqjournal.com/news/state/04224901322newsstate08–04–09.htm on March 19, 2010.

Salisbury, J., & Jackson, D. (1996). *Challenging macho values: Practical ways of working with adolescent boys.* London: Falmer.

Samuelson, R. J. (1997, May 5). The culture of poverty. *Newsweek, 129*(18), 49.

Sánchez, B., Colon, Y., & Esparza, P. (2005). The role of sense of school belonging and gender in the academic adjustment of Latino adolescents. *Journal of Youth and Adolescence, 34*(6), 619–628.

Sanders, M. G. (2000). *Schooling students placed at risk.* Mahwah, NJ: Lawrence Erlbaum Associates.

Sandoval, J. (2002). *Handbook of crisis counseling, intervention and prevention in the schools.* Mahwah, NJ: Lawrence Erlbaum Associates.

Santor, D. A., Messervey, D., & Kusumakar, V. (2000). Measuring peer pressure, popularity, and conformity in adolescent boys and girls: Predicting school performance, sexual attitudes, and substance abuse. *Journal of Youth and Adolescence, 29,* 163–182.

Sappenfield, M. (2002, March 29). Mounting evidence links TV viewing to violence. *Christian Science Monitor.* Accessed at www.csmonitor.com/2002/0329/p01s05-ussc.html on May 20, 2010.

Sattelmair, J., & Ratey, J. J. (2009). Physically active play and cognition. An academic matter? *American Journal of Play, 2*(3), 365–374.

Sax, L. (2005). *Why gender matters.* New York: Doubleday.

Sax, L. (2007). *Boys adrift: The five factors driving the growing epidemic of unmotivated boys and underachieving young men.* New York: Basic Books.

Schriner, C. (2006). *Overcoming stress.* New Delhi, India: Orient Paperbacks.

Schulkin, J. (2004). *Allostasis, homeostasis and the costs of physiological adaptation.* New York: Cambridge University.

Schwartz, D., Dodge, K. A., Coie, J. D., Hubbard, J. A., Cillessen, A. H., Lemerise, E. A., et al. (1998). Social-cognitive and behavioral correlates of aggression and victimization in boys' play groups. *Journal of Abnormal Child Psychology, 26*(6), 431–440.

Senn, T. E., Carey, M. P., Vanable, P. A., Coury-Doniger, P., & Urban, M. (2007). Characteristics of sexual abuse in childhood and adolescence influence sexual risk behavior in adulthood. *Archives of Sexual Behavior, 36*(5), 637–645.

Sennett, R., & Cobb, J. (1993). *The hidden injuries of class.* London: Faber & Faber.

Shaffer, S., Ortman, P. E., & Denbo, S. J. (2002). The effects of racism, socioeconomic class, and gender on the academic achievement of African American students. In S. J. Denbo & L. M. Beaulieu (Eds.), *Improving schools for African American students: A reader for educational leaders* (pp. 19–29). Springfield, IL: Charles C. Thomas.

Sharkey, P. (2009). *Neighborhoods and the black-white mobility gap.* Philadelphia: Economic Mobility Project, Pew Charitable Trusts. Accessed at www.economicmobility.org/assets/pdfs/PEW_NEIGHBORHOODS.pdf on March 19, 2010.

Shaywitz, B. A., Shaywitz, S. E., Pugh, K. R., Constable, R. T., Skudlarski, P., Bronen, R. T., et al. (1995). Sex differences in the functional organization of the brain for language. *Nature, 373,* 607–609.

Shefer, T., Ratele, K., Strebel, A., Shabalala, N., & Buikema, R. (2007). *From boys to men: Social constructions of masculinity in contemporary society.* Cape Town, South Africa: UCT Press.

Shipler, D. K. (2005). *The working poor: Invisible in America.* New York: Random House.

Shipp, S. (2007). Structure and function of the cerebral cortex. *Current Biology, 17*(12), 443–449.

Siedentop, D. (1987). High school physical education: Still an endangered species. *Journal of Physical Education, Recreation and Dance, 58*(2), 24–25.

Sigfusdottir, I. D., Kristjansson, A., & Allegrante, J. P. (2007). Health behaviour and academic achievement in Icelandic school children. *Health Education Research, 22,* 70–80.

Sigman, M. (1995). Nutrition and child development. *Current Directions in Psychological Science, 4,* 52–55.

Silverman, I., Kastuck, D., Choi, J., & Phillips, K. (1999). Testosterone levels and spatial ability in men. *Psychoneuroendocrinology, 24*(8), 813–822.

Slocumb, P. D. (2007). *Hear our cry: Boys in crisis* (Rev. ed.). Highlands, TX: aha! Process.

Slocumb, P. D., & Payne, R. K. (2000). *Removing the mask: Giftedness in poverty*. Highlands, TX: aha! Process.

Snow, C., & Kurland, B. (1994). Sticking to the point: Talk about magnets as a preparation for literacy. In D. Hicks (Ed.), *Child discourse and social learning: An interdisciplinary perspective* (pp. 189–220). New York: Cambridge University.

Snyder, H. N., & Sickmund, M. (2006). *Juvenile offenders and victims: 2006 national report*. Washington, DC: U.S. Department of Justice, Office of Justice Programs, Office of Juvenile Justice and Delinquency Prevention.

Snyder, T. D., Dillow, S. A., & Hoffman, C. M. (2007). *Digest of education statistics*. Washington, DC: National Center for Education Statistics.

Sousa, D. A. (2000). *How the brain learns*. Thousand Oaks, CA: Corwin Press.

Sousa, D. A. (2001). *How the special needs brain learns*. Thousand Oaks, CA: Corwin Press.

Sousa, D. A. (2003). *How the gifted brain learns*. Thousand Oaks, CA: Corwin Press.

Spade, J. Z., & Valentine, C. G. (2007). *The kaleidoscope of gender*. Thousand Oaks, CA: Pine Forge Press.

Spence, C. M., Booth, D., & Walters, E. (2008). *The joys of teaching boys*. Markham, Canada: Pembroke.

Spietz, A., & Kelly, J. (2002). The importance of maternal mental health during pregnancy: Theory, practice, and intervention. *Public Health Nursing, 19*(3), 153–155.

Spinks, S. (Producer). (2002). Inside the teenage brain: Interview–Deborah Yurgelun-Todd [Television series episode]. In T. Mangini (Production Manager), *Frontline*. Boston: WGBH Boston. Accessed at www.pbs.org/wgbh/pages/frontline/shows/teenbrain/interviews/todd.html on March 19, 2010

Springen, K. (2006, May 15). Viagra: Not just for dad. *Newsweek*. Accessed at www.newsweek.com/id/47758 on March 19, 2010.

Starfield, B., Shapiro, S., Weiss, J., Liang, K., Ra, K., Paige, D., et al. (1991). Race, family income, and low birth weight. *American Journal of Epidemiology, 134*(10), 1167–1174.

Stevenson, H. C. (2003). *Playing with anger: Teaching coping skills to African American boys through athletics and culture*. Westport, CT: Praeger.

Stewart, A. J., & Ostrove, J. M. (1993). Social class, social change, and gender. *Psychology of Women Quarterly, 17,* 475–497.

Stocker, C. M. (1994). Children's perceptions of relationships with siblings, friends and mothers: Compensatory processes and links with adjustment. *Journal of Child Psychology and Psychiatry, 35*(8), 1447–1459.

Stueve, A., & O'Donnell, L. N. (2005). Early alcohol initiation and subsequent sexual and alcohol risk behaviors among urban youths. *American Journal of Public Health, 95,* 887–893.

Substance Abuse and Mental Health Services Administration. (2004). *National survey on drug use and health*. Rockville, MD: Author.

Suskind, R. (1998). *A hope in the unseen: An American odyssey from the inner city to the Ivy League.* New York: Broadway.

Svensson, A. K. (1994). Helping parents help their children: Early language stimulation in the child's home. In D. Lancy (Ed.), *Children's emergent literacy: From research and practice* (pp. 79–92). Westport, CT: Praeger.

Swahn, M. H., Bossarte, R. M., & Sullivent, E. E., III. (2008). Age of alcohol use initiation, suicidal behavior, and peer and dating violence victimization and perpetration among high-risk, seventh-grade adolescents. *Pediatrics, 121,* 297–305.

Swaminathan, N. (2008). Study says brains of gay men and women are similar. *Scientific American.* Accessed at www.scientificamerican.com/article.cfm?id=study-says -brains-of-gay on May 20, 2010.

Swan, W., & Dekker, M. (2004). *Handbook of gay, lesbian, bisexual and transgender administration and policy.* New York: Marcel Dekker.

Swearer, S. M., Turner, R. K., Givens, J. E., & Pollack, W. S. (2008). "You're so gay!" Do different forms of bullying matter for adolescent males? *School Psychology Review, 37,* 160–173.

Tannen, D. (1991). *You just don't understand.* New York: Ballantine Books.

Taylor, D., & Dorsey-Gaines, C. (1988). *Growing up literate: Learning from inner-city families.* Portsmouth, NH: Heinemann.

Taylor, S. E. (2006). Tend and befriend: Biobehavioral bases of affiliation under stress. *Current Directions in Psychological Science, 15*(6), 273–277.

Thornberry, T. P., Krohn, M. D., Lizotte, A. J., Smith, C. A., & Tobin, K. (2003). *Gangs and delinquency in developmental perspective.* New York: Cambridge University.

Thorstensen, B. I. (n.d.). *If you build it, they will come: Investing in public education.* Albuquerque, NM: Albuquerque Business and Education Compact. Accessed at http://abec.unm.edu/resources/gallery/present/invest_in_ed.pdf on March 19, 2010.

Thought disorders. (2003). Accessed at www.healthforums.com/library/1,1258,article~4714,00 .html on March 18, 2010.

Thumma, S., & Gray, E. R. (2004). *Gay religion.* Walnut Creek, CA: AltaMira Press.

Tiger, L. (2004). *Men in groups.* Piscataway, NJ: Transaction.

Tokarczyk, M. M. (2004). Promises to keep: Working-class students and higher education. In M. Zweig (Ed.), *What's class got to do with it? American society in the twenty-first century* (pp. 161–167). Ithaca, NY: Cornell University.

Tokarczyk, M. M., & Fay, E. A. (Eds.). (1993). *Working-class women in the academy: Laborers in the knowledge factory.* Amherst, MA: University of Massachusetts.

Trimpop, R. (1994). *The psychology of risk taking behavior.* Amsterdam, The Netherlands: Elsevier.

Turner, J. H., & Stets, J. E. (2005). *The sociology of emotions.* New York: Cambridge University.

Turner, R. J., & Avison, W. R. (2003). Status variations in stress exposure: Implications for the interpretation of research on race, socioeconomic status, and gender. *Journal of Health and Social Behavior, 44,* 488–505.

Turner, V. (1977). *Ritual process.* Ithaca, NY: Cornell University.

Tyre, P. (2006, January 30). The trouble with boys. *Newsweek, 147*(5), 44–52. Accessed at www.newsweek.com/id/47522 on March 19, 2010.

UNICEF. (2007). *Child poverty in perspective: An overview of child well-being in rich countries.* Accessed at www.unicef-irc.org/publications/pdf/rc7_eng.pdf on May 20, 2010.

University of Minnesota. (2009, June 29). Teens who believe they'll die young are more likely to engage in risky behavior. *ScienceDaily.* Accessed at www.sciencedaily.com/releases/2009/06/090629081124.htm on March 22, 2010.

U.S. Army Info Site. (2009). *Joining the army.* Accessed at www.us-army-info.com/pages/enlist.html#ged on March 19, 2010.

U.S. Census Bureau. (2010). *Home page.* Accessed at www.census.gov on May 19, 2010.

U.S. Conference of Mayors. (2008). *2008 economic downturn and federal inaction impact on crime.* Accessed at www.usmayors.org/mayors08actionforums/documents/CrimeReport_0808.pdf on May 20, 2010.

U.S. Department of Agriculture. (2009). *Food security in the United States: Key statistics and graphics.* Washington, DC: Author. Accessed at www.ers.usda.gov/Briefing/FoodSecurity/stats_graphs.htm on March 22, 2010.

U.S. Department of Education. (2008). *A uniform, comparable graduation rate: How the final regulations for Title I hold schools, districts, and states accountable for improving graduation rates.* Washington, DC: Author.

U.S. Department of Education, Office of Educational Research and Improvement. (1994). *TV viewing and parental guidance.* Washington, DC: Author. Accessed at www.ed.gov/pubs/OR/ConsumerGuides/tv.html on March 22, 2010.

U.S. Department of Health and Human Services. (2008). *Child maltreatment 2006.* Washington, DC: Government Printing Office. Accessed at www.acf.hhs.gov/programs/cb/pubs/cm06/index.htm on March 22, 2010.

Valente, S. M. (2005). Sexual abuse of boys. *Journal of Child and Adolescent Psychiatric Nursing, 18*(1), 10–16.

Valeski, T., & Stipek, D. (2001). Young children's feelings about school. *Child Development, 72,* 1198–1213.

VanTassel-Baska, J. (1989). The role of the family in the success of disadvantaged gifted learners. *Journal for the Education of the Gifted, 13*(1), 22–36.

Voyer, D., Voyer, S., & Bryden, M. P. (1995). Magnitude of sex differences in spatial abilities: A meta-analysis and consideration of critical variables. *Psychological Bulletin, 117*(2), 250–270.

Wagner, M., Blackorby, J., Cameto, R., Hebbeler, K., & Newman, L. (1993). *The transition experiences of young people with disabilities: A summary of findings from the national longitudinal transition study of special education students.* Menlo Park, CA: SRI International. Accessed at http://www2.ed.gov/pubs/OSEP95AnlRpt/ch3e.html on May 20, 2010.

Wagner, M., & Oehlmann, J. (2009). Endocrine disruptors in bottled mineral water: Total estrogenic burden and migration from plastic bottles. *Environmental Science and Pollution Research, 16*(3), 278–286.

Wallerstein, J. S. (1988). Children of divorce: Stress and developmental tasks. In N. Garmezy & M. Rutter (Eds.), *Center for Advanced Study in the Behavioral Sciences, Inc.: Stress, coping and development in children* (pp. 265–302). Baltimore, MD: Johns Hopkins University.

Wallerstein, J. S., & Blakeslee, S. (1990). *Second chances: Men, women, and children a decade after divorce.* New York: Tiknor & Fields.

Walpole, M. (2003). Socioeconomic status and college: How SES affects college experiences and outcomes. *Review of Higher Education, 27,* 45–73.

Walsh, F. (2004). The concept of family resilience: Crisis and challenge. *Family Process, 35*(3), 261–281.

Watts-English, T., Fortson, B. L., Gibler, N., Hooper, S. R., & De Bellis, M. (2006). The psychobiology of maltreatment in childhood. *Journal of Social Sciences, 62*(4), 717–736.

Webb, J. T., Amend, E. R., & Webb, N. (2006). *Misdiagnosis and dual diagnoses of gifted children and adults.* Scottsdale, AZ: Great Potential Press.

Wehlage, G. G., & Rutter, R. A. (1986). Dropping out: How much do schools contribute to the problem? *Teachers College Record, 87*(3), 374–392.

Weiman, H. (2004, May 10). *Gender differences in cognitive functioning.* Accessed at http://orion.it.luc.edu/~hweiman/GenderDiffs.html on March 22, 2010.

Weisel, D. L. (2002). *Contemporary gangs: An organizational analysis.* El Paso, TX: LFB Scholarly.

Weiss, L. (1991). *Critical perspectives on early childhood education.* Oxford, England: Routledge.

Weissman, J., Bulakowski, C., & Jumisko, M. (1998). A study of white, black and Hispanic students' transition to a community college. *Community College Review, 26*(2), 19–42.

Whitmore, J. R. (1980). *Giftedness, conflict, and underachievement.* Boston: Allyn & Bacon.

Wiehe, V. (1998). *Understanding family violence: Treating and preventing partner, child, sibling and elder abuse.* Thousand Oaks, CA: SAGE.

Willcox, G. (n.d.) *The feeling wheel.* Accessed at http://guidance.blairschools.dps .schoolfusion.us/modules/locker/files/get_group_file.phtml?fid=3367553&gid =921013&sessionid=139bedd2d549dc75119142a0017af69e on May 20, 2010.

Wilson, J. W. (1990). *The truly disadvantaged.* Chicago: University of Chicago.

Wilson, W. J. (1996). *When work disappears: The world of the new urban poor.* New York: Random House.

Wirt, J., Choy, S., Rooney, P., Provasnik, S., Sen, A., & Tobin, R. (2004). *The condition of education 2004* (NCES 2004–077). Washington, DC: U.S. Department of Education.

Woods, J., & Kingsley, J. (2003). *Boys who have abused: Psychoanalytic psychotherapy with victim/perpetrators of sexual abuse.* London: Jessica Kingsley.

Worrell, J. (2001). *Encyclopedia of women and gender.* San Diego, CA: Academic Press.

Wurmser, L. (1981). *The mask of shame.* Baltimore: Johns Hopkins University.

Xu, J. (2006). Gender and homework management reported by high school students. *Educational Psychology, 26,* 73–91.

Young Adult Development Project. (2008). *Changes in young adulthood*. Cambridge, MA: The MIT Center for Work, Family, and Personal Life. Accessed at http://hrweb.mit .edu/worklife/youngadult/changes.html on March 22, 2010.

Young, R., & Sweeting, H. (2004). Adolescent bullying, relationships, psychological well-being, and gender-atypical behavior: A gender diagnosticity approach. *Sex Roles, 50,* 525–537.

Yowell, C. M. (1999). The role of the future in meeting the challenge of Latino school dropouts. *Educational Foundations, 13*(4), 5–28.

Yowell, C. M. (2002). Dreams of the future: The pursuit of education and career possible selves among ninth grade Latino youth. *Applied Developmental Science, 6*(2), 62–72.

Zill, N. (1993). The changing realities of family life. *Aspen Institute Quarterly, 5*(1), 27–51.

Zimbardo, P. G., & Boyd, J. N. (2008). *The time paradox*. New York: Free Press.

Zins, J., Weissberg, R., Wang, M., & Walberg, H. J. (Eds.). (2004). *Building academic success on social and emotional learning: What does the research say?* New York: Teachers College Press.

Zolotor, A., Kotch, J., Dufort, V., Winsor, J., Catellier, D., & Bou-Saada, I. (1999). School performance in a longitudinal cohort of children at risk of maltreatment. *Maternal and Child Health Journal, 3*(1), 19–27.

Index

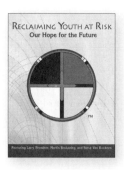

Reclaiming Youth at Risk: Our Hope for the Future
Larry K. Brendtro, Martin Brokenleg, and
Steve Van Bockern
Venture inside schools that have successfully reached youth
at risk. Set includes three 20-minute DVDs and a facilitator's
guide.
DVF011

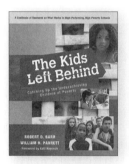

**The Kids Left Behind: Catching Up the Underachiev-
ing Children of Poverty**
Robert D. Barr and William H. Parrett
Successfully reach and teach the underachieving children of
poverty with the help of this comprehensive resource.
BKF432

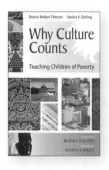

Why Culture Counts: Teaching Children of Poverty
Donna Walker Tileston and Sandra K. Darling
Foreword by Belinda Williams
Afterword by Rosilyn Carroll
Learn how to use students' cultural assets to close the
achievement gap with these research-based methods
of differentiating the context, content, and process of
instruction.
BKF255

**Reconnecting Youth: A Peer Group Approach to
Building Life Skills**
Leona L. Eggert and Liela Nicholas
This award-winning curriculum has been proven effective in
helping high-risk youth achieve in school and decrease their
drug use, depression, and suicide risk.
BKF406

Solution Tree | Press
a division of
Solution Tree

Visit solution-tree.com or call 800.733.6786 to order.